I0421046

Selected Letters of
Sigmund Freud
To Martha Bernays

Selected Letters of
Sigmund Freud
To Martha Bernays

Ankit Patel

Clinical Psychology,
Sardar Patel University, India

Ansh Mehta

Autism & Behavioral Science,
George Brown College, Canada

Selected Letters of Sigmund Freud, To Martha Bernays

Author: Ankit Patel, Ansh Mehta

Copyright © 2015 Ankit Patel, Ansh Mehta

All rights reserved.

ISBN: 978-1-5151-3703-0
ISBN (10): 1515137031
First Published 2015
Price $ 10.28 USD

CreateSpace, Inc
7290 Investment Dr, North Charleston, SC,
United States
Contact Number: +1 843-760-8000, 1-206-508-4011
www.createspace.com

In Association with Amazon
Powered By: The International Journal of Indian Psychology

* * *

All right reserved.
No part of this publication may be reproduced or used in any form or by any means-
photographic, electronic or mechanical, including photocopying, recording, taping, or
information storage and retrieval systems- without the prior Witten permission of author.

Printed in the USA
Title ID: 5626601

Dedication

This Book Is Dedicated To;
Dr. Sigmund Freud, Martha Freud
and all of their family

ACKNOWLEDGMENTS

First and foremost I would like to thank Ernst L. Freud for publishing the book on letters by Sigmund Freud, "Letters of Sigmund Freud" and the Sigmund Freud Museum, London. I would also like to express my gratitude to Tania and James Stern for translating these letters from German to English. The original source for our compilation, "Letters of Sigmund Freud" was published by Basic Books Inc., Publishers, New York. Without these sources, our goal would have been possible to achieve.

I am also thankful to our professor Dr. Suresh Makvana for his guidance and support; to my co-authors who helped me achieve this goal. We also great thankful to Ms. Rinku Methews, Mr. Ajay Chauhan and Mr. Shard Jani.

Lastly I am thankful to the publishers without whom I would not have been able to bring this book to you, Amazon, USA.

PREFACE

The book you are about to read is a result of two students who had the same goal; to understand the relationship between Sigmund Freud and his wife Martha Bernays. We have all heard about Dr. Sigmund Freud, the renowned psychiatrist. But very few individuals have heard of the woman in his life, Martha Bernays. This book is compilation of the letters exchanged between Freud and Bernays between the years 1873 and 1912.

The concept was originated by Ankit Patel who later approached his classmates, the co-author Mr. Ansh Mehta, to help him with his dream of publishing a book focus just on Freud and Bernays.

Along with these letters, we have tried to give a concise version of the relationship between Sigmund Freud and Martha Bernays. The relation between these two individuals was something that cannot be summarized in few pages. However we have tried our best to provide a glimpse of how they felt for each other and what they meant in each other's lives.

We hope that you find these letters of communication as interesting and insightful as we did while we were compiling them. Once you read them, you will get a general idea of the dynamics in their relationship.

Furthermore, among these letters you will also find records of a lot of his major life activities and interactions with other academics in his field. These indeed add to the uniqueness of the commentary that we get on his life and career.

I would like to say that this book would not have been possible without the original source we used for these letters, "Letters of Sigmund Freud". We are grateful that Ernst L. Freud took the time and effort to get his hands on these letters and publishing them.

AUTHOR'S NOTE

The letters in this book have been selected from a previously published book, 'Letters of Sigmund Freud'. In this previous book, the letters were selected and edited by Ernst L. Freud, son of Dr. Sigmund Freud. The original letters were in German; and were translated to English by Tania and James Stern. It was published by Basic Books, New York. The first edition was published in 1960 by Sigmund Freud Copyrights Ltd., London. (Library of Congress Card Number 60-13282)

While the original source consisted of many more letters of communication between Freud and his colleagues and relatives; in this book, we have only selected the selected the letters addressed to Sigmund Freud's wife Martha Bernays; who, at that period, was his fiancée.

I would like to thank the Department of Psychology, Sardar Patel University, Anand for their support and encouragement. Also, I would like to specially thank Ajay Chauhan and IJIP for their extended support and help in producing this book.

Sr. No	Content	Page No.

Freud and Bernays

SIGMUND FREUD

When we speak of psychology, there is no way one would forget Sigmund Freud. Freud was a very prominent psychologist when the field first took birth. Sigmund Freud was born in Freiberg, in a Moravian town called Pribor in the year 1856, 6th of May. Freiberg is now a part of Czech Republic. It is mainly university and mining town. Two years after his birth, his sister was born, Anna Freud. Sigmund also had a brother who passed away in infancy. He was born to Jakob and Amalia Freud.

His father had 2 sons prior to Freud's birth from his first marriage. Jakob's first two sons were named Emanuel (1833) and Philipp (1836). Jakob was a wool merchant and both of Sigmund's parents were of Jewish Galician heritage. Amelia, Sigmund's mother was Jakob's third wife and 20 years his junior. When Sigmund was born, his family was struggling financially and lived in a rented room, in a locksmith's house at Schlossergasse 117.

When Freud was born he had a caul which is a membrane around a new born babies head and face. Her mother considered this to be a lucky occurrence. The family left Freiberg in the year of 1859. Sigmund's half-brothers immigrated to Manchester, England. This resulted in Freud being separated from his childhood playmate of his early childhood, the son of Emmanuel, John. The Freud family first moved to Leipzig and then in 1860 to Vienna. After they moved to Vienna, Amelia gave birth to 4 more daughters (Rosa, Marie, Adolfine and Paula) and a son (Alexander). In 1865, the nine-year-old Freud entered the Leopoldstädter Kommunal-Realgymnasium, a prominent high school. He proved an outstanding pupil and graduated from the Matura in 1873 with honours. He loved literature and was proficient in German, French, Italian, Spanish, English, Hebrew, Latin and Greek. He also liked to read the works of William Shakespeare throughout his life. Some believe that his understanding of human psychology was derived from Shakespeare's plays.

He entered the University of Vienna when he was 17 years old. He planned to study law but instead joined the medical facility at the university; where his studies included philosophy under Franz Brentano, physiology under Erst Brucke and zoology under Carl Claus. He graduated with an MD in 1881.

Freud began his medical career at the Vienna General Hospital in 1882. He did research on the cerebral anatomy which leads to the publication of a seminal paper on the palliative effects of cocaine in 1884. Furthermore his work on aphasia would form a basis for his first book On the Aphasias: a Critical Study, published in 1891. His substantial body of published research led to his appointment as a University lecturer in neuropathology in 1885. He also spent time in the Theodor Meynert's psychiatric clinic.

In 1886, Freud resigned his hospital post and entered private practice specializing in "nervous disorders". The same year he married Martha Bernays, the granddaughter of Isaac Bernays, a chief rabbi in Hamburg. The couple had six children: Mathilde, born 1887; Jean-Martin, born 1889; Oliver, born 1891; Ernst, born 1892; Sophie, born 1893; and Anna, born 1895.

Initially a cigarette smoker, Freud was well known for having a cigar in his hand. According to him, smoking improved his capacity to work and that he could exercise self-control in moderating it. He had received health warnings from a colleague named Willhelm Flies, despite of which, he continued smoking. Eventually he was diagnosed with buccal cancer.

Freud had greatly admired his philosophy tutor, Brentano, who was known for his theories of perception and introspection, as well as Theodor Lipps who was one of the main contemporary theorists of the concepts of the unconscious and empathy.

In his early phase of the career, he was highly influenced by a fellow friend and colleague from Vienna, Joseph Breuer. According to Breuer, when he allowed some of his hysterical patients to talk freely about anything they wanted to; he saw some of their symptoms go away. This influence led Freud to believe that neurotic tendencies of people rooted from past traumatic experiences, but are now forgot or suppressed in the unconscious memory. Together, they published a book on their theories called Studies in Hysteria (1985). However at a later stage Breuer decided to part from Freud because he felt that Freud focused too much on the sexuality of an individual.

Freud also read the works of Friedrich Nietzsche as a student and the analogies between his works and that of Nietzsche could be easily found the moment he started following him. However his interest in philosophy died after he had decided to make a career out of neurology and psychiatry.

The Jewish origin of Sigmund Freud would have a major influence on his works and the formation of his intellectual and moral outlook, as he pointed out in his Autobiographical Study. They would also have a substantial effect on the content of psychoanalytic ideas *"particularly in respect of the rationalist values to which it committed itself".*

Freud got his sense of humour and scepticism from his father, whereas the sentimentalism from his mother. He enjoyed a gratuitous amount of love from his mother, Amalia, who loved to call him 'my golden Sigi.' It is this experience of unconditional love that made him theorize about how your upbringing and love from parents affects your confidence and self-esteem, throughout the rest of your life.

Freud married Martha Bernays in the year of 1886. In the same year he resigned his post at the hospital and started his private practice specializing in 'nervous disorders'. Martha was the grand-daughter of Isaac Bernays, a chief rabbi I Hamburg. Together they conceived six children; Mathilde (1887), Jean-Martin (1889), Oliver (1891), Ernst (1892), Sophie (1893) and Anna (1895).

In the year of 1982, Minna Bernays, Martha's sister, started living with the Freud's at Berggasse 19 after the death of her fiancée. She formed a close relationship with Sigmund which led to rumours about her and Sigmund being involved romantically. These rumours were started by Carl Jung. Later a hotel log was discovered dated 13th August 1898, signed by Freud while travelling with his sister in law; which has been cited as evidence of this affair. One would be wise, however, before believing it completely; as there is no confirmation of this.

Freud continued polishing his theories through the end of 19th century and after period of scientific self-analysis; he published the book Interpretation of Dreams in the year 1900. In 1901 he published another book called The Psychopathology of Everyday Life, and Three Essays on Theory of Sexuality in 1905.

Sigmund Freud was invited to the United States of America to give a series of lectures in the year 1909. After these visits, he published a book on them in 1916, Lectures on Psycho-Analysis.

Around the year 1912, a suggestion was made Ernest Jones during a talk with Ferenczi. In a letter dated 30th July he revealed his intention to form a secret committee of his loyal supporters, which Freud later agreed to. Apart from Jones and Ferenczi, it also included Rank, Sachs and Abraham. It was called 'The Committee'. Later on Eitingon became the 6th member, in 1919. The group was dissolved after 20 years.

MARTHA BERNAYS

Martha Bernays, as you must have figured out by now, was the wife of the Austrian psychoanalyst, Dr. Sigmund Freud. She was born to Emmeline and Berman Bernays on 26th July, 1951. She was their second daughter. Her paternal grandfather Isaac Bernays was the Chief Rabbi of Hamburg.

Martha was raised in an orthodox Jewish environment. Her uncle, Isaac's son, converted to Christianity at an early age and taught German at the University of Munich. The families of Freud and Bernays knew each other since quite some time. In fact Martha's elder brother Eli, married Sigmund's younger sister. However, the Freud family was more liberal. In fact Freud could not stand rituals and religious ceremonies. Martha once told her cousin that –

"Not being allowed to light the Sabbath lights on the first Friday night after her marriage was one of the most upsetting experiences of her life."

Bernays also happened to be the aunt of the Austrian born American publicist and "father of public relations" Edward Bernays.

Martha was a slim and attractive woman at a young age. She was charming, intellectual and properly educated. She also happened to be fond of reading throughout her life. She also happened to be a efficient home-maker; firm but loving with her children. She also tended to be obsessive about cleanliness and punctuality. However some claim that she was not able to form a strong rapport with her youngest child, Anna Freud.

Freud and Martha met each other in the April of 1882 and eventually married on 14th September, 1886. As you will read on, Freud send a lot of letters to Martha while they were engaged. In fact, Freud sent over 900 letters to her, all of which cover the ups and downs of their long distance relationship. Eventually though, they lead a happily married life. After Sigmund's death, Martha dealt with the fact by reminding herself that, "in the 53 years of our marriage, there was not a single angry word between us."

Sigmund Freud and Martha Bernays had six children: Mathilde (1887), Jean-Martin (1889), Oliver (1891), Ernst (1892), Sophie (1893) and Anna (1895).

Time Line of Sigmund Freud

Life Events on Freud' Life

1856 Born in Freiberg (Pribor), northwestern Moravia
1859 Family moved to Vienna's "Leopoldstadt", or second district
1865 Attended high school at "Leopoldstadter Communal-Real-und Obergymnasium"
1873 Registered at the Faculty of Medicine of the University of Vienna
1878 He changed his first name "Sigismund" to "Sigmund"
1881 Obtained his doctorate in Medicine
1882 Worked as a research assistant at the Institute of Physiology under Ernst Brcke
1885 One-year scholarship with Charcot at the "Salpetriere" in Paris
1886 Opened up his first neurologist's office in Vienna, Rathausstrasse 7
1886 Married Hamburg-born Martha Bernays (1861-1951) 1887 Birth of his elder daughter Mathilde (1887-1978)
1889 Birth of his son Martin (1889-1967)
1889 Scholarship in Nancy, with Libault and Bernheim: hypnosis studies
1891 Birth of his son Oliver (1892-1970)
1891 Freud family moved to the house Berggasse 19 in the 9th Viennese District 1892 Birth of his son Ernst (1892-1970) 1893 Birth of his daughter Sophie (1893-1920)
1895 Birth of his daughter Anna (1895-1982)
1895 Publication of his studies on hysteria together with Josef Breuer
1896 Freud called his new therapeutical treatment Psychoanalysis
1900 Publication of the book "Traumdeutung"/ "The Interpretation of Dreams" 1901 Publication of "Psychopathology of Everyday Life"

1902	Appointed associate professor of the Faculty of Medicine at the University of Vienna
1905	Publication of "Der Witz und seine Beziehung zum Unbewuten" und "Drei Abhandlungen zur Sexualtheorie"
1908	Founding of the "Viennese Association of Psychoanalysis"
1909	Guest lectures in the United States, University in Worcester, Massachusetts
1910	Founding of the "International Association of Psychoanalysis"
1912	Publication of "Yearbook of Psychoanalysis"
1913	Publication of the "International Magazine for Psychoanalysis"
1917	Freud comes out with "Lectures introducing Psychoanalysis"
1919	Publication of "The International Journal of Psychoanalysis"
1920	Publication of "Beyond the Pleasure Principle"
1920	Freud is finally appointed Professor of the University of Vienna
1923	Falls ill with palatine cancer
1923	Publication of "The Ego and the Id"
1924	Appointed "Citizen of Vienna" by the City of Vienna
1930	Freud is awarded the Goethe Prize for Literature honoring his "clear and impeccable style"
1930	Publication of "Civilization and its Discontents"
1930	Death of Freud's mother
1933	Freud's book burnt in Berlin
1936	First recurrence of cancer
1938	Nazi Invasion and thus decision to leave Vienna

1938 Journey to London 1939 Inoperable recurrence of cancer
1939 Freud dies on September 23

Books

1891 On Aphasia
1895 Studies on Hysteria (co-authored with Josef Breuer)
1900 The Interpretation of Dreams
1901 On Dreams (abridged version of The Interpretation of Dreams)
1904 The Psychopathology of Everyday Life
1905 Jokes and their Relation to the Unconscious
1905 Three Essays on the Theory of Sexuality
1907 Delusions and Dreams in Jensen's Gradiva
1910 Five Lectures on Psycho-Analysis
1910 Leonardo da Vinci and a Memory of his Childhood
1913 Totem and Taboo: Resemblances between the Psychic Lives of Savages and Neurotics
1915-17 Introductory Lectures on Psycho-Analysis
1920 Beyond the Pleasure Principle
1921 Group Psychology and the Analysis of the Ego
1923 The Ego and the Id
1926 Inhibitions, Symptoms and Anxiety
1926 The Question of Lay Analysis
1927 The Future of an Illusion
1930 Civilization and Its Discontents
1933 New Introductory Lectures on Psycho-Analysis
1938 An Outline of Psycho-Analysis
1939 Moses and Monotheism

Case histories

1905 Fragment of an Analysis of a Case of Hysteria (the Dora case history)
1909 Analysis of a Phobia in a Five-Year-Old Boy (the Little Hans case history)
1909 Notes upon a Case of Obsessional Neurosis (the Rat Man case history)

1911 Psycho-Analytic Notes on an Autobiographical Account of a Case of Paranoia (the Schreber case history)
1918 From the History of an Infantile Neurosis (the Wolfman case history)
1920 The Psychogenesis of a Case of Homosexuality in a Woman, Papers on sexuality
1906 My Views on the Part Played by Sexuality in the Aetiology of the Neuroses
1908 "Civilized" Sexual Morality and Modern Nervous Illness
1910 A Special Type of Choice of Object made by Men
1912 Types of Onset of Neurosis
1912 The Most Prevalent Form of Degradation in Erotic Life
1913 The Disposition to Obsessional Neurosis
1915 A Case of Paranoia Running Counter to the Psycho-Analytic Theory of the Disease
1919 A Child is Being Beaten: A Contribution to the Origin of Sexual Perversions
1922 Medusa's Head
1922 Some Neurotic Mechanisms in Jealousy, Paranoia and Homosexuality
1923 Infantile Genital Organisation
1924 The Dissolution of the Oedipus Complex
1925 Some Psychical Consequences of the Anatomical Distinction between the Sexes
1927 Fetishism
1931 Female Sexuality
1938 The Splitting of the Ego in the Process of Defence

Autobiographical papers

1914 On the History of the Psycho-Analytic Movement
1925 An Autobiographical Study

Analysis of Letters

While compiling these letters, we had a chance to get a unique glimpse of the world Sigmund and Martha shared with each other. The initial letters from Freud to Bernays were before they got married, after their engagement. In these letters we can see that Freud addressed his fiancée as Martha Bernays till the year 1886. They got married in 1886, after which he started addressing her as Martha Freud in his letters.

In each letter Sigmund Freud uses different descriptors to address Martha Bernays. For instance, in letter number 1, he addresses her as *'My precious, beloved girl.'* In letter 2 he writes, *'My sweet girl.'* Other descriptors include *'Fair mistress, sweet love,' 'My sweet little bride,' 'My sweet Marty,' 'Treasured princess,' 'My precious girl,'* etc. In many letters he calls her by the nickname Marty instead of her actual name Martha. This indicates that they shared a close and personal relation and comfort towards each other from early on.

One striking feature of the way Freud wrote his letters was that he never failed to mention the time, date and place from where he is penning the letter. Each letter starts with the city, location, time and date. This tells us that they valued the time of writing the letters as much as they valued the communication itself. In letter 11, he mentions, *'Vienna, 2 a.m., July 13, 1883.'* In letter 15, he mentions, *'Vienna, Sunday, 3 p.m., Sept. 9, 1883.'* We can see that in some letters he writes *'noon', 'night', 'morning'* in place of the actual time on the clock. For instance, in letter 16, he mentions, *'Vienna, Tuesday, at night, September 4, 1883.'* In letter 27, he mentions, *'Vienna, Wednesday evening, December 20, 1883.'*

In almost every letter, Freud informs Martha on his day to day activities; leisurely or work related. For example in letter number 38, he describes his growing friendship with a fellow colleague *Paneth* and how he regrets he might not able to continue it for certain reasons which you will discover as you read the letters. He discusses his plans to support his sisters *Dolfi* and *Rosa* with his money in letter 42.

He also kept Martha Bernays updated on his work related progress and what was going on in his career. In letter 45 he mentions how he was able to acquire a sample of the specimen of his diagnosis which had caused considerable sensation among his friends. He also specifies the arrival of *Dr. Heitler* (Prof. of Internal Medicine at University of Vienna) with whom he planned to develop an instrument for making observations in his experiments. Similarly, in letter 49 he hints at the preparation of his lecture course at the University and the work on brain anatomy.

As you will read these letters, you will come across letters in which he expresses his enthusiasm for the Coca leaf (from which Cocaine is produced) and how he planned to integrate that into his therapies. This was during a time when cocaine was thought to be of a medicinal value rather than the harmful and addictive drug we know it as now.

The letters of correspondence are evidence enough that Freud and Bernays stayed away from each other for a considerable amount of time. However the sheer amount of letters and the content within tells us that even though they were involved in a long distance relationship, they never lost touch with each other or the love they felt for each other.

Almost all letters end with a pleasantry and greetings for Bernays. For instance, letter 57 ends with, 'Greetings and sweet kisses from you Sigmund'. In letter 58 he writes –

"Goodnight, my sweet darling. Its 1:30 am; the day has simply fled by. Hope to work tomorrow. The flowers are for Minna, and I hope there will be a letter for me tomorrow."

Your
Sigmund

In letter 59 he writes—

"Goodnight, my darling, good luck to us and may our dreams come true."

Your
Sigmund

The letters often indicate how Sigmund Freud missed Martha Bernays when they were apart; and how he used to eagerly wait for the day when Martha was expected to visit him in Vienna; where he spent most of his time working. Freud ensured clearing out his schedule for such periods so that he could spend more time with her and not get hindered by other distractions or obligations.

Selected Letters of Sigmund Freud, To Martha Bernays

In these letters, Freud not only focuses on himself or Martha but also on his colleagues and friends. In many letters he describes his relationships with other people and how they are affecting his career. He mentions the new people he met and new contacts that he made while staying in Vienna. The sheer effort in describing each and every detail of his day to day life is admirable and shows us how invested Freud was in his relationship with Bernays. In letter 88 he writes how he won't have time to write to her during his consulting hours as there was too much going on at the clinic and he had a lot of patients. He mentions in the same letter how much money he made that day.

In letter 90, Freud writes how he spends his day in Venice walking, cruising, gazing, eating and drinking. He goes as far as stating how the weather was in Venice while he was there, the sea rough and the atmosphere cool.

After all the letters, we have collected a few pictures of Freud, Martha Bernays and their families and friends. Each picture carries a description of the place and event along with the names of individuals in the photo.

From these letters we can also uncover part of his personality. From his writings we can see that Freud was a romantic and a helpful individual to anyone he knew in his life. He was gracious and generous. We can also see that he had a good command over his language and literature and was a perfectionist in almost every aspect of his life, especially his work and career.

While our initial goal behind compiling these letters to Martha Bernays was to uncover their relationship, these letters also provide a significant amount of insight into Freud's own life and his day to day dealings with his friends and colleagues. As you will see, Sigmund not only focuses on him and Martha in the letters, but he also invariable tells her of his everyday activity. In letter 2, dated June 27, 1882, he tells her of a really minor issue, his pen being stolen from his desk:

"I have torn a few page out of my copy book to write to you while my experiment is taking place. The pen has been stolen from the professor's desk, the people around me think I am computing my analysis; just now someone came over and made me lose ten minutes."

He also kept her updated on his progress as far as his career was concerned. Freud describes a lot of his dealings in his profession with great detail. In letter 21, dated October 9, 1883, he describes how he is busy with paperwork and his research at the laboratory and what his other jobs at the clinic are.

"What I am doing now? I am more industrious than even and feel better than ever. Most of the time I work my way through a mountain of papers, reading partly for myself, partly for the Medical weekly; I sit in the laboratory, where my Method is actually working and looks very fine, although several things still need correcting, and form early in the morning till wards o'clock (I had almost forgotten to tell you) I function in the wards as a Sekundararzt, busy learning writing, and occasionally acting as surgeon."

As you can see, if you read carefully; over and above his relationship with Martha, you can learn a lot about Freud's own life. This is something that you may not find as easily in the biographies of the man. Let us now move on the real thing now, the letters! Hope you find them as insightful as we did.

Selected Letters of
Sigmund Freud

1
To Martha Bernays

Vienna
June 19, 1882.

My precious, most beloved girl

I knew it was only after you had gone that I would realize the full extent of my happiness and, alas! The degree of my loss as well I still cannot grasp it, and if that elegant little box and that sweet picture were not lying in front of me, I would think it was all a beguiling dream and afraid to wake up. Yet friends tell me it's true, and I myself can remember detail more charming, more mysteriously enchanting than dream phantasy could create. It must be true. Martha is mine, the sweet girl of whom everyone speaks with admiration, who despite all my resistance captivated my heart at our first meeting, the girl I feared to court and who came toward me with high- minded confidence, who strengthened the faith in my own value and gave me new hope and energy to work when I needed it most.

When you return, darling girl, I shall have conquered the shyness and awkwardness which have hitherto inhibited me in your presence. We will sit alone in that nice little room again, my girl will settle down in the brown armchair, I at her feet on the round stool, and we will talk of the time when there will be no difference between night and day, when neither intrusion from without nor farewells nor worries shall keep us apart.

Your lovely photograph. At first, when I had the original in front of me I did not think so much of it; but now, the more I stare at it the more it resembles the beloved object; I expect the pale geeks to flush the color our roses were, the delicate arms to detach themselves from the surface and seize my hand; but the precious picture does not move, it just seems to say: "Patience! Patience! I am but a symbol, a shadow cast on paper; the real person is going to return, and then you may neglect me again."

I would so much like to give the picture a place among my house-hold gods that hang above my desk, but while I can display the severe faces of the men I revere, the delicate face of the girl I have to hide and lock away. It lies in your little box and I hardly dare confess how often during the past twenty-four hours I have locked my door and taken it out to refresh my memory.

And all the while I kept thinking that somewhere I had read about a man who carried his sweetheart about with him in a little box, and having racked my brain for a long time I realized that it must be "THE NEW MESLUSINA", the fairy tale in Goethe's Wilhelm Meister's Wanderings, which I remembered only vaguely. For the first time in year I took down the book and found my suspicion confirmed. But I found more than I was looking for. The most tantalizing superficial allusions kept appearing here and there, behind the story's every feature lurked a reference to ourselves, and when I remembered what store my girl sets by my being taller than she is I had throw the book away, half amused, half annoyed, and comfort myself with the thought that my Martha is not a mermaid but a lovely human being. As yet we don't see humor in the same things, which is why you possibly be disappointed when you read this little story. And I would prefer not to tell you all you all the crazy and serious thoughts that crossed my mind while reading it.

These pages, daring Marty, have been written at one sitting. Both yesterday and this evening Eli and Schonberg were here, yesterday in fact several girls as well, and to avoid arousing any suspicion I managed to be quite sociable, although I would far rather have been alone. Only the sight of Schonberg gives me comfort, for the sight of his honest, lively features evokes in me, with sound and color, a host of precious memories. What sorceresses you women are! I like him better by the hour. I got your last greeting from the station and today from Eli the longed-for news of your safe arrival. Your brother seems to like being with us; I have not got to know him much better, as I have not been alone with him since you left. Otherwise I drug myself with work and console myself with the certainty that Martha will remain mine as long as she remains Martha.

My beloved little bride. If at one time I hesitated to bind you to me for life, I would not let you go now even if the most ghastly misfortune befell me and I had to drag you along.

Do please try to steal from your found relations all the photographs of you as a child; it occurs to me that I could have held onto that old photo owned by your mother, at least until your return.

Should you need something from here or want something done, please don't favour anyone but me with your commissions. That is how exclusive I am when I love. Let me know all about all about what you are doing at the moment; it will make it easier for me to put up with your absence. And make good use of your stay in Hamburg for your absence. And make like to see you with those full round cheeks the childhood pictures show.

Now the day has come to an end, the page is covered, and I must check the desire to go on chatting with you. Farewell and don't forget the poor man you have made so bliss-fully happy.

Your
Sigmund

Minna sent me greetings via Schönberg.

2

To Martha Bernays

Tuesday morning in laboratory
June 27, 1882.

My sweet girl

    I have torn a few page out of my copy book to write to you while my experiment is taking place. The pen has been stolen from the professor's desk, the people around me think I am computing my analysis; just now someone came over and made me lose ten minutes. Beside mw a silly panel doctor is testing an even sillier ointment to see if it contains something harmful; in front of me in my apparatus sizzle the gas bubbles which I have to filter. The whole thing once more spells resignation, waiting; two-thirds of chemistry consists of waiting; it is probably the same with life and the nicest thing about it is what one grand oneself in secret, as I am doing now. Your sweet letter came quite unexpectedly and was therefore doubly welcome, and I enjoyed the tall trees and the lovely garden as well as the charming confusion in your dear sentences. Look out, girl, the drawers are being put back in order, I hope, but – I was about to say something else when an utterly idiotic neighbor involved me in a conversation about quicksilver salt. May God punish him for it?

    Well, your letter makes up for today's bad weather; within me the sun is shining from a blue sky, outside there is fog and drizzle. Why do you think the address you used this time is conspicuous? Here it is the most convenient, or do you mean it is conspicuous in Wandsbek? Your letter (I am no longer going to say "sweet", I am going to apply to the Berlin Academy for an increase of affectionate adjectives – I am so in need of them) bore the postmark Hamburg. Is Wandsbek that near? Have you seen the sea yet? Please give it my best regards-we will meet yet. May land and sea cooperate to keep my girl flourishing and make her stay in foreign parts a pleasant one. I am so conceited I no longer want to recognize them as her home. How bold one gets when one is sure of being loved!

    Poor Minna had to invent a five-page letter on the spur of the moment. What are those dangerous thing Marty wrote to her? Let me know what Eli write about me. It must be rather funny.

You are now even making me lazy, Marty. I do work all day, but in the evening I am quite incapable of looking at a book. Fiction I do not care for; I know a beautiful fairy tale which I have experienced myself, and as for lofty science I bow low and say; "Your Highness, I remain your humble, most devoted servant, but please don't hold it against me; you have never looked kindly upon me, never said a comforting word to me; you don't answer when I write to you, listen when I speak, but I know another lady to whom I mean more than I do to you, who repays my every service a hundredfold, and who moreover has but one servant and not, like you, thousands. You will understand if I now devote myself to the other undemanding and gracious lady. Keep me in pleasant memory until I return. I have to write to Martha."

I expect this will change when I can see and speak to Marty every day. The two ladies will get along well together and the proud, unapproachable one will have to be willing to pay the taxes for the lovely, modest one.

Yesterday I went to see my friend, Ernst v. Fleischl, whom hitherto, so long as I did not know Marty, I envied respect. But now I have an advantage over him. I believe he has been engaged ten or twelve years to a girl of his own age, who was prepared to wait for him indefinitely, but with whom he was now fallen out, for reason unknown to me. He is a thoroughly excellent person in whom nature and education have combined to do their best. Wealthy, skilled in all games and sports, with the stamp of genius in his manly features, good-looking, refined, endowed with many talents and capable of forming an original judgment about most things, he has always been my ideal, and I was not satisfied until we became friends and I could properly enjoy his value and abilities. On this occasion I brought him a criticism of a pamphlet by him, he taught me the Japanese game "Go" and astounded me with the news that he was learning Sanskrit. I had to promise him to keep this a secret, but I knew at once that for Martha this had as little validity as other and more important secrets. Then I looked around his room, fell to thinking about my superior friend and it occurred to me how much he could do for a girl like Martha, who was enchanted even by our humble Kahlenberg, would admire the Alps, the waterways of Venice, the splendor of St. Peter's in Rome; how she would enjoy sharing the importance and influence of this lover, how the nine years which this man has over me could mean as many unparalleled happy years of her life compared to the nine miserable years spent in hiding and near-helplessness that await her with me. I was compelled painfully to visualize how easy it could be for him—who spends two months of each year in Munich and frequents the most exclusive society—to meet Martha at her uncle's house. And I began wondering what he would think of Martha. Then all of a sudden I broke off this daydream; it was perfectly clear to me that I could not relinquish the love one, even if to be with me were not the right place for her. A part of the happiness Martha renounced in the hour of our engagement we will make up for later. My girl must promise to keep young and fresh as long as possible, and even after nine years to be so charmingly surprised by everything new and beautiful as she is now. Martha will not allow herself to be absorbed by household worries, Martha is not a Lisette. Can't I too for once have something better than I deserve? Martha remains mine.

A fond greeting to the dear one

From
Sigmund

3
To Martha Bernays

Vienna, Friday
July 14, 1882

Fair mistress, sweet love,

I beg leave to inform you that your gracious letter wherein you allow me to take a pilgrimage to your fair eyes hath made me mighty happy and that I am packing my satchel in order to learn if it be merely a found glance I can expect from you or a kiss from your lips as well. And in so far as a traveler and stranger enjoys all manner of privileges and rights, you must not take it amiss if I desire more than one. Remember the words of an Anglo- Saxon poet who invented many gay and sad plays and himself acted in them, one William Shakespeare:

> *Journeys end in lovers meeting,*
> *Every wise man's son doth know*

And how he goes on to ask:

> *What is love?' tis not hereafter;*
> *Present mirth hath present laughter;*
> *What's to come is still unsure:*
> *In delay there lies no plenty;*
> *Then come kiss me, sweet and twenty,*
> *Youth's a stuff will not endure.*

But should you not understand these frolicsome lines, consult none other than A.W. Schlegel's translation of Twelfth Night; or, what you will.

So if it pleaseth you let us descend from the lofty art of poetry to common prose and allow your servant to tell when he hopes to be near you. Your brother Eli hath amicably stretched out a helping hand with a free ticket as far as the frontier of this empire. Thereafter beginneth the realm of poverty, as the man of your choice hath more claims to the kingdom of heaven than to the treasures of this earth. Cannot therefore carry on as I commenced and if turn my back on this town at the hour of 8 on Sunday morning; you must not expect me in your Hamburg before Tuesday at 5:46 in the afternoon. Can even be that I arrived later, for railway complexities are a hard little nut for my weak head to crack and none of our other allies knows how to find a way out of such an entanglement of trains. After I have refreshed and washed myself in the early morning so that you will not take me for a Moor, I shall hasten to Wandsbek where enemies are holding you in- I trust uncertain- safekeeping. Allow me to hope that you will still be in the grave, for I would so much like to greet you unwitnessed by other human eyes. You have omitted, alas, to inform me about the length of the road and means of conveyance as well as your presence in the grove, but perhaps you will do so in your letter which I expect tomorrow.

Once we have seen each other the future will take care of itself and I will write no more about it.

If your cousin Max will prove himself a friend and conduct you into town, I will be eternally grateful to him, although by so doing he would only be fulfilling an ordinary obligation toward mankind. Hope, however, he will not consider that three id company; he certainly will not find any support for his love of company from your uncompanionably lover and will be asked in a friendly manner to leave us alone. Do not care to kiss you beneath the gaze of a stranger, and would not know what to say to you in his presence. He will not be able to deny that he owes it to humanity to leave us alone.

So that you may be warned about your lover, you must not expect to make a great parade of him. He wears an unsightly shapeless gray jacket, light-colored breeches, will today acquire a gray felt hat like that of your brother but of less value . Your brother's travelling bag holds as little linen as is consistent with a man's property; as for the greatcoat, you have frequently sanctified it with your touch. You also know the ungainly walking stick, the wallet with your picture, the finger with the ring on it, to all of which has been added a little heap of money to support us in your inhospitable native town. May suffice to introduce ourselves as an engaged couple to the sun which brings everything to light, and to produce a likeness for our younger brother's sisters. A gem lies in wait for your birthday, keeps catching my eye as I go by, but I do not dare to acquire it now and bring it along; it will have to wait here unit August 4. Thus your knight errant will bring nothing but his loving heart, he will come without weapons, having left poison and dagger at home for a rival. He cannot wait to see you and tell you how devoted he is and that if need be he is ready to protect and defend you against friend and foe. You know already that he was pleased to come off well spare him any hostilities by an honest renunciation.

Oh, this wretched medieval style, today but never again! I feel so much like a knight errant on a pilgrimage to his beloved princess who is being kept prisoner by her wicked uncle. You must have been rather bored by it, sweet Marty; be tolerant. If you only knew how mad things look within me at the moment. But I will arrived in a quite sensible condition. To my joy, darling, Schonberg has returned.

Once again a kiss on credit, my angle once again; perhaps tomorrow I can write from Mödling, then cash payment.

To our happy reunion.

Your
Sigmund

4
To Martha Bernays

Tetschen, Sunday, 8 o' clock
July 16, 1882

My sweet little bride

If you only knew how lovely it is here and how incomparably more lovely it would be with you! The Elbe flows by, still a modest little river, showing me the way to you, to you. High mountains, some overgrown, some bare in strange formation, nice little houses which do not look as though they were meant to be lived in but to be put up and knocked down as in a game of bricks, all in a row along the river, a few proud buildings gazing down from the mountain slopes as though they had nothing to do with the rest. Once of them all by itself on a hill, a castle or a monastery or something like that- it's really all the same to me. On the left lies Bodenbach, on the right Tetschen and between them two bridges, one for the railway and the other for "vagrant scholars" on their way to their sweethearts. On the second bridge I had to pay a toll of to Kreutzer, but this I did willingly; I was glad I had not broken a leg. I have been telling such an awful lot of lies lately. I crossed the bridge to Tetschen because in Bodenbach there was no coffeehouse from which I could write to you. It turns out that I have to stay here till 2 A.M. and won't reach Hamburg until 2:30 P.M. on Tuesday and don't know if I can see you even on Tuesday , and I am completely roasted or grilled- no, not completely done, only half, like an English roast beef. But to return to Bodenbach. There is a kind of holy Sunday stillness over every-thing and the bells are ringing, I don't quit know why, and the streets are so clean, the people so polite, the old ones looking as I have always expected Christian Fürchtegott Gellert to look and the younger one so modest, as if nowadays they themselves lived in of God. In the middle of the market place there is a square stone, could be the tomb of an Old Saxon King, but it probably isn't and I really don't care what it is. It is enough that I can walk around here without being asked, "Who gave you the ring you're wearing on your finger?" No, this I am not going to take off till I am once more under restraint in Vienna. I was about to tell you that I was bent on finding a coffeehouse. And then I saw in the street a round, rosy-cheeked girl and I asked: "Fair lady"- not: "Let it not offend you," etc., but:"Could you tell me where I can find a coffeehouse?" And imagine, I was standing right in front of it, and the girl was the waitress or the proprietor's daughter. And here I am, the only guest, in a little room with several chairs and tables; it takes a quarter of a century to get a coffee and there is very little sugar with it; my Marty will have to give more sugar in my coffee. But the cake is good- I am eating two slices, spend – thrift I am- one for Marty, and now I must hurry up and stop or I will have to leave all my money behind in the coffeehouse: for light and link and use of the furniture, and all the beautiful things I still have to stay will have to be left unsaid. But we are going to compete as to who will set eyes on Martha first: I or this scribble. We will be travelling by the same train, and then the happy time begins, the great unique happy time of being with the beloved, which is so near at hand, and I am already getting used to the idea of having experienced it, because I just couldn't believe it and all along have felt the fear of which the poet sings:" Earth, sink not down," etc.

But farewell now, sweet Marty.

Good bye
Your blissful lover
Sigmund

5

To Martha Bernays

(Hamburg) Sunday
July 23, 1882

"The Jew is called Nathan. (A strange Jew- H'm!) Continue, Worthy Nathan.(Or something like that; I can't go to the public library just now to verify the quotation. The man in the Cansemarket3 will forgive me.) This was the beginning of our acquaintance. I had Suddenly grown very fond of a little girl and suddenly found myself in Hamburg. She had send me a ring which her mother had once received from her father; I had a smaller copy of this ring4 had stayed with her after all, for everyone who saw and spoke to her loved her, and this is the sing of the true ring. I didn't like this much and I wondered for a long time how I could make her less attractive, so that no one would fall in love with her any more until one day it occurred to me that what mattered was whether she loved several people, not whether several or everyone Love her. Once this idea had occurred to me I was very happy in Hamburg. The mornings were always warm and beautiful, the evenings seemed close to the morning, and I was grateful to the to the day for filling the gap between the beautiful morning and beautiful evening. True the tyrannical temperament that makes Little girls afraid of me could not be subdued. I wanted exclusiveness, and since I had attained it in great and important matters, I strove to achieve it in small and symbolic once. My Girl came from a family of scholars, and wrote- for the time being only letters- with untiring hand, thus spending the little money she had on notepaper. So I decided to acquire some notepaper for the dear industrious child and chose some on which she could write to me only. An M and an S intimately entwined, the generosity of engravers grants us, render every page useless for intercourse save between Marty and me. The man from whom I ordered this despotic paper on Friday could supply it only Sunday; " For on Saturday," said he, " we are not her. It is one of our ancient customs." (Oh, I know that ancient custom!) He was a jovial old gentleman whom I took to be fifty-four; with this error I won his heart, as not long before I had won another heart with another error. He was seventy- four years old and boasted of his capacity for enjoyment and work and declared that he had intention of departing from this life so soon. I liked the man. I happened to be in a similar mood. On Sunday I saw him again. He was very proud of the elegance of the monogram, but he did not wise to treat me as a mere customer. He showed me the building of the Deutsche Bank opposite his shop.

"That where the merchants of Hamburg keep their money which they don't want to leave at home; these cellars are full of gold-and silver." I expressed the hope that one vein of this rich metal deposit reached as far as his shop. But merchants invariably dissimulate. He then explained why so many people swarm into this building. If you were to owe me   some money; he said instead of paying me in cash, it would be transferred in the bank from your account to mine. I felt uneasy; apart from being in debt, I know absolutely nothing about banking. But he would not let me go, I had to take a chair beside him while he questioned me as to where I had already been, and recommended to me this and that excursion; "I'd like to come along with you myself, but I am an old Jew, and just look at me." I looked. His beard was shaggy. Yesterday they were not allowed to be shaved. "You know, of course, which Fast day is upon us ?" I knew all right. Just because years ago at this season (owing to a miscalculation) Jerusalem had been destroyed I was to be prevented from speaking to my girl on the last day of my stay. "But what's Hecuba to me? 5 Jerusalem is destroyed and Marty and I are alive and happy. And the Historians say that if Jerusalem had not been destroyed, we Jews would have perished like so many races before and after us. According to them, The invisible edifice of Judaism became possible only after the collapse of the visible Temple. So, said my old Jew, nine days before Tisha B'av6 we deny ourselves every pleasure. We here are a number of men of the old school all of whom adhere to our religion without cutting ourselves off from life. We owe our education to one single man. Years ago Hamburg and Altona formed one Jewish community, later they separated; until the Re-from movement came to Germany, instruction was carried out by inferior teachers. Than it was realized that something had to be done, and a certain Bernays was called and chosen to be Chancham.7 This man has educated us all.- The old Jew was about to embark on his achievements, but I was more Interested in Bernays the man. Was he from Hamburg? No he came from Wurzburg, where he had studied at Napoleon's expense. (Oh, the myth- forming power of mankind!) He came here as a very young man, thirty years ago he was still living her. Did you know his family? "Me? I grew up with the sons."

I now remembered two names, Michael Bernays in Munich, Jacob Bernays8 in Born.

That's they, he confirmed, and there was also a third son,9 who lived in Vienna, and died there.

I also knew something about this third brother, whose name remained so much in the background.

The father's rich talents were divided among the sons, the old man continued. The father had been a linguist, an interpreter of the scriptures, and had left behind him some distinguished children. Thus one son chose languages, the material of which became the scientific work of his life, the second one is still teaching the appreciation of the subtleties and the wisdom which our great poets and teachers have put into their writings. The third son, a serious, reserved man, dealt with life on a level even more profound them is possible for science and art: he was above all a human being and created new treasures instead of interpreting old ones. Glory to the memory of him who presented me with my Marty!

Imagine if my old Jew, Who was now talking with such enthusiasm about the teachings of his master, could have guessed that his customer, allegedly a Dr. Wahle10 from Prague, had this very morning kissed the granddaughter of his idol! He went on to recall the memories of his own youth, and traits of Nathan the Wise now began to appear in what he said. Bernays had been a quite extraordinary person and had taught religion with great imagination and humaneness. If someone just refused to believe anything well, then there was nothing to be done about him; but if someone demanded a reason for this or that which was looked upon as absurd then he would step outside of the and justify it for the unbeliever from there. Take the law about food, for example: what could be less important than what one eats? To which he would say: Let us back to the story of Creation. A fable it may be, but what the whole of mankind has believed for centuries surely cannot be nonsense; it must have meaning. When God had created the first human beings and put them in the Garden of Eden, Was not the first commandment he gave them a commandment about eating? From this tree mayest thou eat, but not from that one. Why was it not a command about morals? And if the first commandment God made one about food, can it be of no importance what one eats?

My old Jew provided several more ingenious attempts of this kind to explain and support the Scriptures. I knew the method: the Holy scriptures' claim to truth and obedience could not be supported in this way, there was no place for reform, only for revolution; but in this method of teaching lay enormous progress, a kind of education of mankind in Lessing's sense. Religion was no longer treated as a rigid dogma, it became an object of reflection for the satisfaction of cultivated artistic taste and of intensified logical efforts, and the teacher of Hamburg recommended it finally not because it happened to exist and had been declared holy, but because he was please by the deeper meaning which he found in it or which he projected into it. Was criticism, even though willfully manipulated and directed toward definite aims, but well suited to give his disciples the decisive direction which my old Jew was still following while I was fetching our monogram for the granddaughter of his master.

His teacher, he continued, had been no ascetic. The Jew, he said, is the finest flower of mankind, and is made for enjoyment. Jews despise anyone who lacks the ability to enjoy (I couldn't help thinking of what Eli, to his credit, once disclosed about his philosophy when in his cups: *homo sum.*) The law commands the Jew to appreciate every pleasure, however small, to say grace over every fruit which makes him aware of the beautiful world in which it is grown. The Jew is made for joy and joy for the Jew The teacher illustrated this with the gradual importance of joy in the holy days

At New Year the Christian says: Let us hope we have a better time in the new year than in the old. For the Jews first comes Rosh Hashana, when the lots are drawn for the whole year. It is then that We have reason to fear the divine decision: this is the feast of the fear of God. At Yom Kippur we fast all day to show our love of God; only love can bring such a sacrifice. This is the day dedicated to the love of God. But then comes Succoth, of which it is written: "The Jew must be only joyful during these days, and one day is called the Joy of the Law. This is the Day dedicated to the Joy in God."

A customer arrived and Nathan became a merchant again. When I took my leave I was more deeply moved than the Old Jew could possibly guess. If he ever came to Prague, he said, he would give himself the pleasure of looking me up. He won't find me in Prague, but as a substitute I will offer him another pleasure. If my Marty wishes to take with her to Vienna some gifts in the form of notepaper, she must go to the Adolphsplatz, to our old Jew, disciple of her grandfather, and mention her name. Let him see that the stock of his master has not deteriorated since he sat at his feet. And as for us, this is what I believe: even, if the form wherein the old Jews were happy no longer oilers us any shelter, something of the core, of the essence of this meaningful and 1ife-affirming Judaism will not be absent from our home.

Your
Sigmund

6
To Martha Bernays

Vienna, Monday
August 14, 1882

My sweet Marty

I found no leisure to write to you all day today, so this has to be once again a nocturne, anyhow it is quite a while since there has been one. As you know, the poor human being is always more affectionate in the evening than in the morning, because, because well, there are so many reasons that I don't need to mention even one.

My precious darling, for the first time in ages we have been to the Prater1 again-we, the family, not the Band2. We were invited by our old man3 in order to make up for some less good days, When. he isn't exactly grouchy, which alas is very often the case, he is the greatest optimist of all us young people. The day aroused memories pleasant in themselves, but melancholy m then recurrence. Here lt was that we had been close to each other every day and every day had grown fonder of each other; here we had all eaten and drunk beer together and finally we had even pressed each other's hands and I had not been able to wait for the moment to get up, which would give me my girl again, and on the whole I had been so shy and had kissed my Marty so rarely because as yet I could not quite grasp what has now become the first and most natural condition of my life: that I had suddenly won for myself a Unique, incomparable girl. Oh, the Prater is a paradise Indeed; only the Wandsbek grove is more beautiful because there We were alone like Adam and Eve, except for a number of animals (Which were harmless enough): gentle, venerable clergymen, inquisitive yet discreet old women and some useful animals, too- cows which gave milk, and waitresses who produced butter and cakes, etc. Eve wore a brown dress as befitted the changed conditions and a great big hat that never wanted to stay on and the Almighty had placed seats under the lovely tall trees, all of which Were ours, and nowhere to be seen an angel with a flaming sword, only one little delicate angel with emerald eyes and two sweet lips which, refusing to remain closed, had to be closed with kisses and yet were kissed so rarely just because it was morning--and, yet all in all so perfectly beautiful, but even more beautiful bound to come. Are you already thinking of the day you are to leave, it is no more than a fortnight now, must not be more or else, yes, or else my egoism will rise up against Mama and Eli-Fritz and I will make such a din that everyone will hear and understand. And when you do return you are coming back to me, you understand, no matter how your filial feelings may rebel against it. From now on you are but a guest in your family, like a jewel that I have pawned and-that I am going to redeem as soon as I am rich. For has it not been laid down since time immemorial that the woman shall leave father and mother and follow the man she has chosen? You must not take it too hard, Marty, you cannot fight against it; no matter how much they love you, I will not leave you to anyone, and no one deserves you, no one else's love compares with mine.

What is it like in Wandsbek? Does anyone still remember your "admirer"? Are people turning up claiming to have seen you with him? You were so delightfully daring, my adorable girl. Will you be willing to take some risks here, too? You simply mustn't be as rash here as you were there, for that I could never ask, but now and again, when we haven't seen one another for a long time, you will be able to think something up, won't you?"Oh, don't let's talk you, what if I am compelled to think about it all the time? Are you enjoying the choral contest4 and are you turning the ring around a little less often? Well, there has to be ebb and flow in Hamburg Here no longer.

Today I gave myself a clean bill of health and tomorrow am going to start work. Short steps and a long way, but We Win get there all right, and then we will be able to wander on, arm in arm. How lovely that will be!

If only I knew what you are doing now. Standing in the garden and gazing out into the deserted street? Ah, I am no longer passing by to press your hand, the magic carpet that carried me to you is torn, the winged horses which gracious fairies used to send, even the fairies themselves, no longer arrive, magic hoods are no longer obtainable, the whole world is so prosaic, all it asks is: "What is it you want, my child? You shall have it in time. "Patience is its only magic word. And in saying so forgets how things get lost when we cannot have them then and there, when we have to pay for them with our own youth.

Good night, my beloved Marty
Forever
Your
Sigmund

7

To Martha Bernays

Vienna, Thursday
August 17, 1882

My beloved girl

A month ago today my delighted eyes spied you sitting on the veranda of the Philipp's house and you didn't recognize me, and two months ago you had just become my fiancée. Since then little, very little has happened to make the union for which we are striving a reality. And yet we have made some use of this time. We were strangers to one another, had to get to know each other, experience things together- this we have achieved; and if we both keep healthy and some demon does not disrupt our feelings for one another, the ensuing monthly memorials should find us well on the way toward our longed-for goal. For you, poor darling, hope for the future must compensate you for the many sacrifices you are imposing on yourself at the moment; for me, the courage to court you has already found reward in the awareness of my sweetest good fortune. If I may repeat a request today, please don't be taciturn or reticent with me, rather share with me any minor or even major discontent which we can straighten out and bear together as honest friends and good pals. I have always acted like this, sometimes at the expense of your delicate nature, and you have told me that you agree. If in doing so I must have often hurt your feelings, I know you have not misunderstood my efforts to make you my own as intimately as possible, and if this be egotistical, love after all cannot be anything but egotistical.

It is only the reflex of my usual wretched mood that makes me talk of such things, for just now there aren't any disagreements between us and I am not afraid of any, nor for that matter of any be so powerless to prove my love for you; but so long as you believe in me and love me- and both I know to be true- there is no doubt that we will both remain fit and capable of enjoying better times. Don't scold me for being serious, Marty; you know I can be gay when you are with me. With found greetings and in restless anticipation of this beastly month soon vanishing into the past.

Your
Sigmund

8
To Martha Bernays

Vienna, at night
August 18, 1882

Why do I o'er my paper once more bend?
Ask not closely, clearest one, I pray:
For, to speak truth, I've nothing now to say;
Yet to thy hand at length' twill come, dear friend.
Since I can come not with it, What I send
My undivided heart shall now convey,
With all its joys, hopes, pleasures, pains, today:
All this hath no beginning, hath no end.

My beloved girl

A friend, normally a hardened sinner with whom I am fond of commiserating on the absurdity of this world, suddenly turned soft today; and, striding into the next room, took from the bookcase Master Goethe's incomparable poems and read out to me some lines of such ardent emotion (which had more meaning for me than for him) that I had to run away in order not to betray myself and to be alone with my thoughts. This afternoon I could not return to work and soon ran into another friend whom I used to know at the University and who since then has been diverted by a sad misfortune from his original aims. Contact with friends hold for me nowadays a special charm- the seriousness of life seems to have disclosed itself to us almost simultaneously; what in the beginning seemed to u dear and desirable, but easily accessible, has now withdrawn into the far distance although still remaining dear, and perhaps some of them carry, as I do, a new cherished aim locked up in their hearts. Dejected as I am, weary and looking as I do with so little hope into the future, I nevertheless cannot think of a soul with whom I would like to change places; I still haven't lost faith in myself, and as for Marty, my Marty what could anyone have to offer in her stead?

We are all poor promise to help one another whenever we can. They are all decent fellows, or I would not have them as friends; we can do so little for one another, and yet I rarely leave any one of them without feeling that he has helped me, that the interest he takes in me, the hope he places in me, have lifted me out of my despondency, have offset some part of the injustice done to me, and that perhaps I have been able to do the same for him. Although not so blissful as the knowledge that one is loved by an exceptional girl, I would not renounce that feeling that so many men stand quietly by me and help me to live! It also helps me to accept the fact that we are so poor. Just suppose, darling girl that success corresponded precisely to the merit of the individual, would not love tend to lose some of its purity? I would not be sure whether it were me you loved or the recognition given to me, and if misfortune befell me the girl could say: I do not love you any more, your unworthiness is proven. It would be as horrible as in the world of uniforms where everyone wears his merit written on his collar and chest. But since fortune's manner of rewarding or ignoring merit is so capricious- and unjust- love may remain faithful to the poor man without becoming false, and if I seem insignificant and unimportant to other people, with you I am allowed to feel rich and to enjoy unlimited praise and recognition.

Oh, my darling Marty, how poor we are! Suppose we were to tell the world we are planning to share life and they were to ask us: What is your dowry?- nothing but our love for each other.- Nothing else?- Now it occurs to me that we would need two or three little rooms to live and to eat in and to receive a guest, and a stove in which the for our meals never goes out. And just think of all the things that have got to go into the room! Tables and chairs, beds, mirrors, a clock to remind the happy couple of the passage of time, an armchair for an hour's pleasant daydreaming, carpets to help the housewife keep the floors clean, linen tied with pretty ribbons in the cupboard and dresses of the lasted fashion and hats with artificial flowers, pictures on the wall, glasses for everyday and others for wine and festive occasions, plates and dishes, a small larder in case we are suddenly attacked by hunger or a guest, and an enormous bunch of keys- which must make a rattling noise. And there will be so much to enjoy, the books and the sewing table and the cosy lamp, and everything must be kept in good order or else the housewife, who has divided her heart into little bits, one for each piece of furniture, will begin to fret. And this project must bear witness to the serious work that holds the household together, that object to a feeling for beauty, to dear friends one likes to remember, to cities one has visited, to hours one wants to recall. And all this, a small world of happiness, of silent friends and proofs of lofty human values, is as yet only in the future; not even the foundation of the house has been laid, there is nothing but two poor human creatures who love one another to distraction.

Are we to hang our hearts on such little things? Yes, and without hesitation, so long as some event beyond our control does not knock on the silent door. And of course we will have to go on telling each other every day that we still love each other and can find neither the means nor the time to let the other know, who wait until some misfortune or disagreement extorts an affirmation of affection. One must not be mean with affection; what is spent of the fund too long, they diminish imperceptibly or the lock gets rusty; they are there all right but one cannot make use of them. Oh, at the moment there are not even two poor human being who love each other. Only one is here, the other is far heart. The poor sweet child, who has already suffered so many sad things which she doesn't mention, and hardly was she able to breathe again when she gave herself to the poor luckless man, renouncing so willingly her own little share of life's pleasures. But you have got to bring me luck, for me you are luck itself, without you I would let my make use of them to gain our share in this world so as to enjoy it with you.

You have my most affectionate greetings; perhaps at this moment you are thinking of me; it is the hour when you used to wait for me in the garden.

**Your
Sigmund**

9

To Martha Bernays

Vienna
September 25, 1882

For my beloved Marty

I am beginning these notes without waiting for your answer my girl, in order to tell you more about myself and my activities than our personal contact would allow. I am going to be very frank and confidential with you, as is right for two people who have joined hands for life in love and friendship. But as I don't want to keep on writing without receiving an answer I will stop as soon as you fail to respond. Continuous inner monologues about a beloved person that are not corrected or refreshed by that person lead to false opinions about the mutual relationship, and even to estrangement when one meet again and finds things to be different from what one had thought. Nor shall I always be very affectionate, sometime I will be serious and outspoken, as is only right between friends and as friendship demands. But in so doing I hope you will not feel deprived of anything and will find it easy to choose between the one who values you according to your worth and merit and the many who try to spoil you by treating you as a charming toy.

Please don't think, my sweet darling, that I have any wish to find fault with you. On the contrary, all I want is that there should be no touchiness and no secrets between us. You know that from the moment we entered into this alliance we both had to change to some extent in order to become for each other what we wish the old Marty does not seem to have given way completely to my beloved girl.

"So he is not satisfied with me" you will think and- shed a tear? No, you won't . Because we must face all this as equals. Would I shed a tear if you remonstrated with me? We have taken upon ourselves a difficult task and in carrying it out we must support and correct one another. Words of love alone cannot do this; living together does not mean hiding unpleasant things from one another or glossing over them; helping one another means sharing everything that comes along. It seems to me that up to now all of you have demanded and expected only pleasure things from friendship. You have all been quite content if you could end up by saying: He or she was so nice and pleasant today. In August when I wasn't well and Eli came to see me, he asked me reproachfully why I- begin so seriously ill!- didn't go to the hospital instead of being a burden to my family. This want to spend only pleasant hours with you, all I want is to keep feeling and adjust to each other as far as is possible for two human being.

I hope for my part I shall succeed. There was one instance in which you were not quite fair to me and offended me deeply; it was when you refused to drop your "friendship" with Fritz Wahle for my sake. I was fully conscious that you nobly kept your independence and truthfully reported everything to me. You will eventually agree with me more fully on this point. You were not quite sure enough in your judgment; let us both hope that such thing will never happen between us again. And you will understand me when I say that even for a beloved girl there is still one further step up: to that of friend, and that it would be a ghastly loss for us both if I were compelled to decide to love you to hide my thoughts and opinions- in short, the truth. Please accept the hand which I hold out to you in fondest affection and confidence and do with me as I am doing with you.

Your
Sigmund

10

To Martha Bernays

Vienna, Thursday
October 5, 1882

To whom else but to my deeply beloved, most ardently worshiped Martha should I report on the outcome of my visit to Prof.Nothnagel?1 Don't be cross, my lovely girl (whose charm at noon today is still confusing me), if I initiate you into the intricate byways and conditions to which my struggle for existence has brought me. It is after all not just my battle and interest, we 'are So intimately connected, I am so unspeakably happy that you are mine, so certain of your interest, that everything becomes important to me only when you share it, Even if the outcome was not exactly what I had desired, it was nevertheless quite honorable and I see no reason to abandon hone for a better future so long as you, my angelic girl, can put up with me.

Well, I went to see N. with my collected works and a recommendation from Meynert. The house he lives in is new, hardly finished, the flat reeks of varnish, the waiting room simply magnificent. On the wall hangs a picture showing four children, a beautiful boy who in twenty years will be snatching the best jobs from the medical students, a little girl with hints of potential beauty for whom within ten years the young men. Will be fighting at students' balls: both with brown hair from which I concluded, rightly as it turned out, that their mother is dark; then elder girl unattractive blonde with her father's features, holding in her arms a baby of in indeterminate sex. Soon I also found on the walls books written by the father of this promising brood, a large portrait of a serious, dark-haired woman on an easel-like contraption, and standing beside her the man who holds our fate in his hands. It gives one quite a turn to be in the presence of a man who has so much power over us, and over whom we have none. No, he is not one of our race. A Germanic cave man. Completely blonde hair, head, cheeks, neck, eyebrows, all covered with hair and hardly any difference in color between skin and hair. Two enormous warts, one on the cheek and one on the bridge of the nose, no great beauty, but certainly unusual. Outside, I had felt a bit shaky, but once inside, as usual in "battle," I felt calm.

"I have been asked to bring you greetings from Prof. Meynert and to express his regrets having missed you the other day. And on my own behalf I am taking the liberty of handing you this card."

While he was reading the card, I sat down. I knew what was on it: "Dear Professor, I am herewith warmly recommending to you Dr. Sigmund Freud on account of his valuable histological work and would be grateful if you would give him a hearing. In the hope of seeing you soon. Yours-Theodor Meynert." –

"I set great store by recommendation from my colleague" Meynert. What can I do for you, Herr Doktor?"

When speaking, he made a very pleasant impression; he talked like a man who means what he says and who weighs his words, reserved but trustworthy.

"You've probably guessed already," I said. "It is known that you're about to engage an assistant, and it is also long you will have a new job to offer. I also understand that you set great store by scientific research. I have done a certain amount t I have no opportunity to Continue, so I thought it advisable to present myself as an applicant."

"Have you some off prints of your papers with you, Herr Doktor?"

"Yes," said I, putting my hand in my pocket.

While he was glancing through the papers, 'I explained my position. "At first I studied zoology, then I changed to physiology have done some research in histology. when Prof. Brücke told me he couldn't give his assistant notice and advised me, a poor man, not to stay with him, I left."

Now N. began. "I won't conceal from you that several people have applied for this job, and as a result I can't raise any hopes. It wouldn't be fair, I will mention you as a candidate, however, and put your name down in case another job turns up, As I've said, I won't make any promises, but this you will hardly have expected. *Qui vivra verra.* I'll hold onto your papers, if I may."

All this was said in a friendlier manner than I can reproduce here; he was not so gruff, if anything rather reserved in a friendly way. One thing emerged clearly: the first job, to be occupied immediately, has been taken (by a son of a Prague professor, so rumor has it); as for the second, not yet vacant, he does not want to commit himself, but he did take me seriously.

'"One more thing," I said. "At the moment I'm serving as an Aspirant in the General Hospital, and if you "can't offer me any hopes or prospects of an assistants job, I could serve as an Aspirant with you.

"What exactly is an Aspirant?" he asked. "I'm not yet familiar with the terms used here."

I now gave a brief explanation (something my girl must also bear with here) to the effect that a hospital consists of two things: clinics and departments-clinics, -where the professor and his assistants teach the students; departments, where the *Prinarius* and his a *Sekundarii* (without students) treat the patients. The professor has the choice of his assistants, but the *Primarius* cannot choose his *Sekundarii.* Any doctor can become an Aspirant while waiting for the position of a *Sekundarius* to fall vacant, and during this time he is called, as I am, Aspirant. This interim period, however, can be spent in a clinic as well as in a department. Understand, Marty? Professor N. did not appear to understand entirely, for he - said; "If you have any prospects of a job as a surgeon's assistant (which I haven't); then don't hesitate to accept. But I advise you to go on working in the scientific field, and when it's time to hand in an application, I will consider your case.

"But I cannot afford to go on working in the scientific field in this way, I've got to branch out and go 'through the .medical curriculum as fast as possible in order to Set myself up in practice, probably in England, where I have relations. I have worked long enough for nothing. As it is, I've got to abandon a chemical papers which I had started."

"I am not referring to publications," he replied. "Just go on working in the scientific Held; after all, medicine can be practiced scientifically, too."
"I know that, and it differs little from the working methods of the physiologist."
"It's the same," he interrupted.
"But I feel I must pursue what is most necessary for the medical practitioner.
"Do that, it won't prejudice you in my eyes when the opportunity turns up."

"If I understand you correctly then, I am to act as though there won't be any hope of my working with you in the immediate future?"

"Exactly," he said. "Take what you can get; I can't promise' you anything, it wouldn't be fair. Incidentally, are you thinking of deciding on an academic or a practical career?

My inclinations and my past experience point toward the former, but I've got to-"
"Of course, first you've got to live. Well, I'll keep you in mind. one more. Qui *vivra verra*. And with that he got to his feet.

In any case, I thank you very much. And may I come and fetch my papers after a while? They are my only copies."

"I'd like to read' them. Could you come and pick them up in three or four' Weeks? I'm very busy at the moment"

"I can quite believe it, Professor. As a matter of fact, the gist of what I've written can be found in the annual report and in Schwalbe's *Neurology*."

One more bow, and that was that. Well, my girl? For the moment all this has led to nothing. The first job is gone, and for the second my application will certainly be Considered, for the man spoke honestly. In a few days Meynert, for whom N. has great respect, will intercede personally for me, and if he gets to know the other friends I have among the professors, I will rise in his estimation. For the time being, however, I shall go on working as though. there is no hope. what I am going tackle next I am not quite sure. I am considering dermatology, not a very appetizing field, but for general practice very important and interesting in itself. I intend calling at that department tomorrow; if there are no Aspirant jobs vacant, I shall go to Meynert.

I hope from now on to be on better terms with your poor mother, whom I like despite our conflicting interests, and you I hope to see at 10 A.M. on Saturday in the prater.

Your faithful
Sigmund

11
To Martha Bernays

Vienna, 2 A.M
July 13, 1883

Gardener Bünsow, lucky man, to be allowed to be allowed to shelter my darling sweetheart! Why didn't I become a gardener instead of a doctor or writer? Perhaps you need a young chap to work for you in the garden, and I could offer myself so as to bid good morning to the little princess and perhaps even demand a kiss in return for a bunch of flowers.

But this letter is not to Gardened Bünsow, rather to you, my Marty , my longing to know, daring? Your sore throat will be better, is bound to be better, by the time you get this letter-it was nice of you to write to me about it, but not at all nice of you to nice of you to write to me about it, but not at all nice of you to get it. If it's nothing worse, don't let yourself be excessively coddled, wrapped in shawls and all that kind of thing, my child; I believe that a little toughening, which can surely be risked in such harmless circumstances, is better in the long run. And I am looking forward to your news and hope you will eat, if necessary in secret, and if you need money for this my sweet, just let me know, for I have some again.

Today was the hottest, most excruciating day of the whole sea-son, I was really almost crazy with exhaustion. Realizing that I was badly in need of refreshment, I went to see Breuer, the poor man, and was taking salicyl. The first thing he did was to chase me into the bathtub, which I felt rejuvenated. My first thought on accepting this wet hospitality was: If Marty were here, she would say, "This is just what we must have too" Of course, my girl, and no matter how many year it will take, we shall have it, but the only miracle had supper upstairs in our shirtsleeves (at the moment I am writing in a somewhat more advanced négligé), and then came a lengthy medical conversation on moral insanity and nervous diseases and strange case histories-your friend Bertha Pappenheim also cropped up-and then we became rather personal and very intimate and he told me a number of things about his wife and children and asked me to repeat what he had said only" after you are married to

Martha." And then I opened up and said: "This same Martha who at the moment has a sore throat in Düsternbrook, is in reality a sweet Cordelia, and we are already on terms of the closest intimacy and can say anything to each other." Whereupon he said he too always calls his wife by that name because she is incapable of displaying affection to others, even including her own father. And the ears of both must have been ringing while we were thinking of them with serious tenderness.

But now found greetings, for I have gone to sleep, Marty.

Your
Sigmund

12

To Martha Bernays

Vienna, at night
August 22, 1883

My beloved Marty

I have little more to say in answer to your letters than that I am delighted with all the good news they contain, that I readily agree with you in every respect, that I would prefer to tell you all I think with a kiss and on the whole-glancing back-can't we claim to now become lasting and deep?

I will use this later hour to tell you some factual news, otherwise these little items accumulate and I will be able to drop back into a light and intimate chat.

Well, today I heard from Simon that he has instructed his bank to remit to Anna 100 florins to buy herself something for the wedding. It is none of my business, but this really isn't much from a rich uncle, nor is it very delicately given. If we even get rich, sweetheart, we will do things differently. I know that you for one won't need any encouragement.

Paneth wrote today out of his dream of bliss; he sends greetings to you and his bride to me, the whole thing a panegyric to this best of all possible worlds.

Since Holländer left I see only two friends-Herzig, who occasionally comes in from the country where the girls also are, and Robert Franceschini, a friend as yet unknown to you, who began studying medicine with me- there were only three in the whole of our class to take up medicine, and we scribbled our names on a skeleton which we bought together- he then had to abandon medicine and zoology on account of a protracted illness, then became tutor to some rich people whom he also had to leave because of his illness, and finally after some improvement he found a job as a railway official. At the moment he is living very modestly with his old mother, writes feuilletons under the initials R.F. for all the papers on all kinds of subjects, in which he is helped by his numerous talents and his erudition. Lately he has embarked on the study of philosophy and is writing a thesis to take his degree. But the only person one can be with and talk to intimately is Herzig, whose value you know or at least can guess. On Tuesday for the first time we went to the electricity exhibition, just to find our bearings, for we intend to revisit it frequently. Everything is as yet unfinished, noise and uproar from the machines which are partly still in the process of being set up, no light as yet, However, we have acquired the available books on electricity and are busy studying them. So far I haven't seen anything especially interesting except a row of small room containing, under the pretext of electric lighting, some charming furniture, as well as a very nice exhibition by Jaray. The sight of these rooms made me lose all my philosophy. Herzig remained cold and said he had already finished that chapter, knowing he would never own such things. I was in ecstasy, imagining your delight at sight of these lovely furnishings. I think I guessed: Oh, if only I could I could marry a man who would give me that! I envied the young ladies this beautiful dream and was sad at the thought that my girl, on seeing all this, would not be able to look so hopefully into the future. I was quite glad you weren't there. This mood soon passed, however, and I fell to thinking more sensibly: how unhappy we could be on this splendid sofa and how happy in an old leather armchair, and that the wife should always be the most beautiful ornament in the house, and that all these room were empty and lifeless because their mistress wasn't there.

What we see on future visits to the exhibition will be faithfully reported to you.

During these past few days I have been having some serious differences of opinion with Pfungen, and I have treated him too harshly, which was very unfair of me. I am afraid I do have a tendency toward tyranny, as someone recently told me, and added to this is the fact that I am all too gay nowadays; I let myself go in a kind of youthful high spirits of immaturity, which used to be quite alien to me. I also have the capacity, in other respects praise-worthy, of hating someone on intellectual grounds, just because he is a fool, and this is what the otherwise excellent man unfortunately is. He is quite *meschugge* and all his thoughts are crazy. But I must alter my attitude toward him, for he is really a very decent man.

This same kind of gay moodiness, as I would like to call it, also leads to my making good use of my time: I read a lot, fritter away much of the day. For instance, I read a lot, fritter away much of the day. For instance, I now possess Don Quixote, with Doré's large illustrations, and concentrate more on it than on brain anatomy. You are quite right, little princess, it is no reading matter for girls, I had quite forgotten the many coarse and in themselves nauseating passages when I sent it to you. No doubt it achieves its aim in a remarkable manner, yet even this is some-what remote from my princess. But the incidental stories are charming, all these you really must read. While in the midst of the book today I nearly spilt my sides; I haven't laughed so much for ages. It is so beautifully done.

Now farewell, my lovely princess. In my silence about our love please see once more the symptom of my unworried and healthy certainty of possession, and go on loving me as I will always love you, and then we will compete as to which of us can be the more loving.

With affectionate greeting till we write again
Your
Sigmund

13
To Martha Bernays

Vienna
August 23, 1883

Treasured princess

Just back from my country practice to find your sweet letter with the good news that you are feeling well and all the pleasant things you don't tire of telling me every day. I had a talk today with a colleague in the hospital, Dr. Widder, who said he considers it a great mistake to marry as long as one has no money and that it will take me eight years to get anywhere. All this he was saying not from worldly wisdom, etc. but out of the innocence of his heart, as he sees it. Defending my case valiantly, I told him he just doesn't know my girl, who is willing to wait for me indefinitely, that I would marry her even if she had turned thirty – a matron, he interrupted - that I would bring it off by starting work elsewhere, that a man has to take some risks and that what I stand to gain is worth any risk. He admitted that within two years I could be earning two thousand gulden, and showed me a letter from a Dr. K. in Brünn, who hopes to earn five to six thousand florins in the course of a year, etc. He was not entirely serious about the gloomy picture he painted. The most beautiful part of it all I of course did not tell him – that one so unspeakably happy to feel oneself loved, even if we don't yet belong to each other formally and completely, and above all if one is lucky enough to have abducted a little princess! Courage, my treasure! You will become my wife much earlier and you won't have to feel ashamed of having had to wait so long. One quite small piece of good news I will let you know today: unless I am very, very much mistaken I think my "latest method" is going to work; I wrote to you before that I am putting my hope in the light of the sun – it really seems to be effective; discovery requires patience and time and luck; If something is to succeed it always has to start like this. So courage, my little princess.

My patient is no worse; I am busy dispelling all kinds of minor complaints; so far nothing has happened that I cannot cope with, and when I give an order I often hear that Breuer has contemplated doing the same. His wife, of whom you have, my angel, but is not quite so sweet; I admire her because she has excellent observation, nurses him with such patience and is so good at cheering him up. I really do hope he will improve; Breuer doesn't think he will, and fears the next six years of slow deterioration.

So you have run out of notepaper, Marty? In September you shall have a slice of my salary and with it order some more notepaper of the same kind. No , no, rather spend it on yourself, it is such ages since you have had any money, and at the moment I cannot send you more than a few little marks, but I can't exchange them today, in fact not before Saturday, as tomorrow I am on duty.

Now I must break off for the evening, I will continue this letter to my beloved at night.

Forgive me, dearest, if I so often fail to write in a way you deserve, especially in answer to your affectionate letters, but I think of you in such calm happiness that it is easier for me to talk about outside things than about ourselves. And then it seems for me to talk about outside things than about ourselves. And then it seems to be a kind of hypocrisy not to write to you what is uppermost in my mind: I have just spent two hours – it's now midnight – reading Don Quixote, and have really reveled in it. The stories of the indecent curiosity   of Cerdenio and Dorothea, whose fate is interwoven with Don Quixote's adventures, of the prisoner whose story contains a piece of Cervantes' life history – all this written with such finesse, color, and intelligence, the whole group in the enchanted tavern is so attractive, that I cannot remember ever having read anything so satisfactory which at the same time avoids exaggeration. All the happy couples, the ladies who promptly love one another like sisters and receive the poor Moorish girl so affectionately, the knight lashed to the window and ordered to prevent wicked giants from breaking in : none of this is very profound, but it is pervaded by the most serene charm imaginable. Here Don Quixote is placed in the proper light through being no longer ridiculed by such crude means as beatings and physical maltreatment but by the superiority of people standing in the midst of actual life. At the same time Sancho, with his sly motives and in the way he keeps tumbling from the dream world into reality, is wonderful. And then Dore's illustrations; they are superb only when the artist approaches his sub words of the tavern –keeper's wife to show how a wretched little knight has cut in half six giants with one blow of his sword, the lower halves of the bodies still standing while the upper halves roll in the dust. This picture is really of a marvelous absurdity and a splendid contribution toward dispelling all the romantic nonsense about chivalry. He succeeds too with the Oriental scenes, the strange and grandiose architecture, also with the harshness of nature in the dark mountains; and he is good wherever the text lends itself to caricature, for instance when the ghosts bewitch the knight and lock him up in a cage. It's enough to make one die with laughter. But in other scenes, those in which the true character of the knight is revealed, the subtle irony is missing. Here the caricature is mostly exaggerated and the illustrations fall far short of the text. But I can well imagine how magnificent his illustrations for *Orlando Furioso* must be, material that would seem to be made for Dore, even several things out of the Bible, especially the legendary and heroic scenes.

Now, my dearest most beautiful sweetheart, please take these comments in your stride, don't consider me ungrateful or reproach me for thinking too little of you or seeming too cool. The more intimate your letters become, the more silent I get; as I read them something like a continual tacit assent goes on within me; yes, that is how I want my Marty to be, as she is now. Long may she remain this way and healthy to boot.

Well, I wonder what you got for your birthday? And what does Minna mean by saying that you had three this year? I am afraid you have been treated rather poorly by me this time. Just wait, though, till things are going well with me, and I will celebrate your birthday properly. We have after all so many dates to celebrate, I have seen you on so many days – and often wasn't grateful enough – and the memory of having seen you is quite enough to make a memorial of the occasion.

Goodnight, my princess, keep well and remain fond of

Your
Sigmund

Please thank Minna for her sweet, intelligent letter which can only receive a less brilliant answer, for which she won't have to wait very long, however. Ask her to stop writing Schonberg for once, so that he can answer me, too.

Am I so sleepy or is it just that my handwriting is so bad today? I can hardly read it. I even omit words, too, don't I? One more affectionate greeting, Marty

14

To Martha Bernays

Vienna, Tuesday night,
August, 28, 1883

My Precious girl

I came to my patient today completely at a loss how to find the necessary sympathy an attentiveness for him; I felt so limp and apathetic. But this feeling vanished when he began to complain and I to realize that I have a function and an influence here. I don't think I have ever attended him with greater care, nor made such an impression on him; work really is blessing. And now I feel well and clam; I have decided to be severe with myself so as not to fall back into such a state of weakness; the awareness of calm preparedness is surely the finest thing a man can find in himself. It is what the poet described in the lines:

New strength and heart to meet the world incite me,
The woe of earth, the bliss of earth, invite me....

The mood for which an even greater port found the loftiest expression with the words:

Let us consult
What reinforcement we may gain from hope;
If not, what resolution from despair.

But I have no use for this mood, it must not be spent on one decisive battle, rather be saved for a long, tenacious struggle with small, isolated tasks.

I am well again now and able to enjoy things and am glad that even in the bad days I did not think of you with any less tenderness than I do now. There may easily be a more accommodating love than mine for you, but hardly a more serious one, in cold blood. When I am angry with you nowadays, as I was about the traveling project, it is gone as soon as I have spoken my mind, and I don't like to leave it unspoken, for it all burrows its way into me and cannot be cauterized away, proofs of which you have had. But – then no more about me – introspection and presumption are also part of this mood.

It wasn't very easy to find any peace today; the moment I got home I was told that my mother had waited two hours for me, left a small parcel and a message for me to go to the

Prater as Father is leaving tomorrow.. He is not leaving till tomorrow evening. I cannot stand anyone's company for long, least of all that of the family; I am really only half a person in the sense of the old Platonic fable which you are sure to know, and the moment I am not active my cut hurts me. After all, we already belong to each other and if we are going to have a tussle – this too is part of love –let it be at close quarters.

What else happened today? Oh yes, my bookseller came to see my advice whether he should accept a book which the author himself wishes to translate from the original English. Since my bill with him is pretty big, I am glad to establish a personal relationship with him. The book is beautifully illustrated and I am going to recommend it to him. I hope he will present me with a copy of the translation. Unfortunately it is not something I can send to you, it is a pathological histology! Oh, my precious sweetheart, what stupid, uninteresting things I write to you! I am going to tell you a funny little story, but you mustn't be sorry for me. When I got home I found a letter from a friend who frequently comes to see me(privately), asking me to lend him another gulden till the first of the month, to leave it with the janitor and if I don't have a whole gulden, then half a gulden, but at once; on the first everything would be paid up. Well, my entire fortune happened to consist of four – Kreutzer, which I couldn't very well offer him. So I decided, since my ordinary bankers were not at home, to waylay a colleague who owes me some money, in fact quite a considerable sum for this time of month. But he couldn't be found, I was getting hungry and had to go to Prater, so what was I to do? Then fortunately another colleague appeared from whom I borrowed a gulden in no time. But by then it was too late to send part of it to the other friend, I just had to go to the Prater, so today he got nothing, but if my debtor pays tomorrow he shall have something. One day he and I will probably be rich, but don't you think this is a funny kind of gypsy life, Marty? Or does this sort of humor not appeal to you and make you weep over my poverty? Don't take it to heart; before you have a chance to sell your jewels to save me I shall be an affluent man again.

And now goodnight, sweet princess; if I have written more impersonally and less affectionately, I have a little purpose –and you are to guess what it is.

Your faithful servant
Sigmund

15

To Martha Bernays

Vienna,
Wednesday evening
August 29, 1883

My beloved Martha,

Your charming, intelligent letter and your excellent description of the Wandsbek Fair gave me great pleasure and suited my continuous improvement –if there weren't still catarrh I could say my well – being. You think almost like Wagner in Faust during that beautiful walk and I ought to answer with gentle indulgence in the manner of Dr. Faust: "Here I am Man –dare man to be!" But no, beloved, you are quite right, it is neither pleasant nor edifying to watch the masses amusing themselves; we at least don't have much taste for it anymore and our anticipated or already enjoyed pleasures, an hour's chat nestling close to one's love, the reading of a book that lays before us in tangible clarity what we think and feel, the knowledge of having achieved something during the day, the relief of having solved a problem –all these gratifications are so different that it would be affection to pretend that one really enjoys the kind of spectacle you describe.

But now please forgive me if I quote myself; I remember something that occurred to me while watching a performance of Carmen: the mob gives went to its appetites, and we deprive ourselves. We deprive ourselves in order to maintain our integrity, we economize in our health, our capacity for enjoyment, our emotions; we save ourselves for something, not knowing for what. And this habit of constant suppression of natural instincts gives us the quality of refinement. We also feel more deeply and so dare not demand much of ourselves. Why don't we get drunk? Because the discomfort and disgrace of the after-effects gives us more "unpleasure" than the pleasure we derived from getting drunk. Why don't we fall in love with a different person every month? Because at each separation a part of our heart would be torn away. Why don't we make a friend of everyone? Because the loss of him or any misfortune befalling him would affect us deeply. Thus we strive more toward avoiding pain than seeking pleasure. And the extreme cases are people like ourselves who chain themselves together for life and death, who deprive themselves and pine for years so as to remain faithful, and who probably wouldn`t survive a catastrophe that robbed them of their beloved. Our whole conduct of life presupposes that we are protected from the direst poverty and that the possibility exists of being able to free ourselves increasingly from social ills. The poor people, the masses, could not survive without their thick skins and their easygoing ways. Why should they take their relationships seriously when all the misfortune and society have in store threatens those they love? Why should they scorn the pleasure of the moment when no other awaits them? The poor are too helpless, too exposed, to behave like us. When I see the people indulging themselves, disregarding all sense of moderation, I invariably think that this is their compensation for being a helpless target for all the taxes, epidemics, sicknesses, and evil of social institutions. I am not going to pursue this thought any further, but it would be easy to demonstrate how "the people" judge, think, hope, and work in a manner utterly different from ourselves. There is a psychology of the common man which differs considerably from ours. They also have more community spirit than we have; only for them is it natural that one man continues the life of the other, whereas for each of us the world comes to an end with our death.

My dearest girl, if you dislike this kind of talk, just tell me to stop. You don`t realize the extent of your influence over me and you must not conclude from the harsh way I deal with certain things connected with the basic conditions and experiences of our relationship that I am generally intolerant. I am quite prepared to be completed by the person one loves, if only we had got as far as that, Marty!

The girl in whose fate I took such an interest lost the moving effect she had on me after a few days. There were too many complications involved which did not correspond to our own relationship, and too many faults on her side. Being a physician certainly doesn`t make one immune to human suffering, nor should it, but one does become less vulnerable if their happiness in one`s own life…

I find myself in continuous professional friction with Pfungen, and have now got to the point where I contradict him in front of Meynert; he of course backs me up, because Pfungen is full of delusions and eccentric ideas. But I must admit to myself that I do have a tyrannical streak in my nature and that I find it terribly difficult to subordinate myself. I am sure you know this already, but if you love me in spite of it I shall manage to be happy all the same.

I am spending every free hour of the day on my paper, the beginning of which is not unsatisfactory. I don`t think, Marty, that I react to success and failure quite as excessively as you make out. I am not yet quite clear about my method; it works, but I am not always in control of it, it does not always produce the same results.

Goodnight, my sweet darling, my precious princess, you. Your letters cheer me up tremendously.

Go on being fond of
Your
Sigmund

16
To Martha Bernays

Vienna, Tuesday, at night
September 4, 1883

My dearest girl,

I can well imagine why I have had no letter from you today. Two days ago you got the news that I was quite ill again, and being worried, you decided to wait for the next letter; I wrote that letter four days ago, but today I am quite well ad want to discuss travelling plans with you. Not in your direction alas, my sweet child, for I am not rich enough for that. Actually, since I cannot come to you I have a good mind to drop the whole idea; but listen to this and tell me what you think. I have two invitations on hand: the one to go and visit Brust in Baden; I met him today in town, he had come in with his brother; also intends to call at the Kaiser Josef Strasse. I could stay eight to ten days-travelling expenses one golden, living expenses there not more than here; Brust even wants to try to introduce me at the inn at his brother as he did two years ago so that the waiters won't accept any tips from me but that I will not tolerate this year.

The other suggestion is rather more original: Dr. Widder insists that on the fifteenth I accompany him for a fortnight to his native village, near Kaschau, where to plan is to do nothing but eat grapes. I would be the guest of his family; the journey cost fifty to sixty florins, but as I should be travelling as an *Oberarzt* I would pay only half, and very likely I could even get a free ticket via Zuckerkandl as far as Pest, so I could save even more. So all in all, it would cost me ten florins more than I spend here in a fortnight, but I would also have seen Pest, the Carpathians, and lead a regular gypsy life oblivious of medicine for ten days. The second suggestion has a lot to recommend it, but involves an expense of time and money, which the first does not. Now which one shall I decide on? I grant you a decisive vote and will enumerate the circumstances which I must take into account. First, Breuer must be back and take K off my hand, then the letter must have paid up, and everything depends on whether the fee is nearer thirty or fifty. Second, Breuer may have some suggestion which could be either useful to me or which I wouldn't be able to refuse. At the moment, then, it is difficult to know what to do. Marty, I have just had a crazy dream: suppose K were to reward my efforts for the month of August by paying me one hundred golden, then I could leave Baden here and Kaschau there and travel to Wandsbek. Alas, my good girl, there is no hope of this. He would have to pay me seven florins a visit. Oh, if only I had cured him: why on earth didn't I do that? And by the way, we still haven't agreed on the conditions for our reunion.

But to be serious again, my dearest treasure, I think I will accept one of the two invitations. Although endowed with a very strong constitution. I Have not been in a continuously good condition these last two years; there have been so many hardships that it really required the joy and happiness of our relationship to remain healthy. I am like a clock that hasn't been repaired for a long time, dusty in every joint. As my miserable person has taken on a greater importance, also for myself, since I acquired you, I am more concerned with my health and do not intend to wear myself out. I would rather renounce my ambition, attract less attention, have less success, than endanger my nervous system. In the future, for the remainder of my apprenticeship in the hospital, I think I shall try and live more like the Gentiles-modestly, learning and practicing the usual things and not striving after discoveries and delving too deep. My happiness lies above all in my relations with you, later in making you mine. We must stick close together and make life beautiful for ourselves, and what we need for our independence we will achieve by decent, steady work without any gigantic efforts.

Once we are together and have strengthened and assured each other, then will be the time to aim at greater things again. Why aren't you here, darling, to give me your answer? I am afraid I do waver a lot in my plans, don't I? Please tell me, and what you are thinking and how you want things to be.

Schönberg was supposed to come today, but he hasn't, perhaps Brust's visit prevented him. And what are you doing, my silent sweet heart-but you are not silent, you are only far away and won't be able to answer this until September 8. I have wanted to send you a paper, a special number of the Illustrated, but I have no money yet, still haven't been relieved in Pötzleinsdorf. The poor man isn't at all well, but I did finally succeed in getting him to sleep; to comfort a wife with lies is so hard.

Today I met Frau Emma Oppenheim with a child, on a bench in the Gersthofer Allee; this time I recognized her earlier. I thought to myself how strange it is that Hamburg children are wafted over here and the Viennese over there.

Farewell my dear sweetheart

Your faithful

Sigmund

17
To Martha Bernays

Vienna, Saturday
September 8, 1883

My precious Marty

What can it be that you want and do not dare to mention? I am so filled with curiosity, especially since Schonberg tells me there is something similar on his horizon. What on earth can it be, then? A tooth out of the Caliph's jaw, a jewel from queen Victoria's crown, a giant's autograph, or something equally fantastic which would mean putting on my armor at once and setting out for the Orient?

Or is my sweetheart's desire nearer home; could it possibly be a deed of self-conquest? Am I to fast at Yom Kippur or reconcile myself to someone I don't like? Surely not My Martha would not abuse her power and persuade me to actions that lack sense as well as honesty. I hope she wants something for herself and I hope I can catch it and give it her.....

My greatest concern at the moment is to get Schonberg away for the winter; one of his brothers is making difficulties; I am waiting for the arrival of the other to see what I can do; there's even a vague possibility of his going to the Riviera as a tutor independent of the brothers. But I think I might be able to do something with the brothers. Your confession about your reading, princess, amused me greatly. It seems as though you don't quite want to bite- like the peasant in the old proverb: "What he doesn't know he won't eat."

But do finish Don Quixote; the second part contains many fewer of the shocking qualities than the first and is far more fantastic. I also quite agree that in winter, or when the weather begins to get bad, you should write only every other day, so as to get some unclouded happiness. But Marty, You will then have to write a little more every other day, otherwise I might develop an uncontrollable hunger for news of you.

I now no longer have to choose and you don't have to decide about that journey; Dr. Widder can't get away on the fifteenth because his chief is no vacation and he is in charge of the department. What actually makes me hesitate about Baden is whether, considering B's ambiguous attitude toward Rosa, it is a good idea to get on such intimate terms which could be interpreted as speculating on future relations. Or do you think this is too far-fetched? I am very well, by the way, and very pleasantly stimulated. Breuer is not back yet; I am expecting him with impatience, for personal and professional reasons; the weather is now so bad that he can't very well stay away much longer. I have an idea he will turn up on Monday.

I can see quite clearly from your letters that you are well, but please tell me also what you look like, whether you have put on weight, whether you are feeling better and if your complexion is clearer than when you left- or else, or else I will ask Minna, or, having sold my library, I will come and waylay you in the grove, just to convince myself, and go off again the same evening. Would you like me to do that, my darling? And what about the cold baths; is it again too for them?

Affectionate greetings to my precious sweetheart from
Your devoted
Sigmund

Best regards to Minna; I am going to compose a long letter to her in the near future.

18
To Martha Bernays

Vienna, Sunday, 3 P.M.
Sept. 9, 1883

My sweetheart

Don't you even again say that you are cold and cannot find the right word; you write such unspeakably sweet, such movingly tender letters that I could answer them only with a long kiss, holding you lovingly in my arms. I hope one day it will be nothing but a pleasant memory when I tell you know I have yearned for you and I will never quite believe it when I really have you with me. I daren't think much about it for that my patience to bear it till then would melt away.

Now, in answer to all your dear questions, let me point out that I am not such a sick man as you think. Since those bad days that were more of an interruption of health than an actual illness, I feel very well; the inactivity suits me for a short time, and if nothing comes of the Baden project I am not to be pitied; as for Kaschau, it is off, as you will know today. I only mean to renounce the exhausting pursuit of distinction and, as you say, keep myself productive and capable of enjoying our life together. I have always thought that there is a short and a long way of achieving something; if the short one is barred to me I will confidently take the long one, and this is precisely what is happening to me at the moment. I was enchanted to learn that you are so ambitious for me, my sweet child; in the beginning , I wasn't; I was seeking in science the satisfaction which the effort of searching and the moment of discovery offer; I never was one of those people who can't bear the thought of being washed away by death before they have scratched their names on the rock amidst the waves. But when I think what I would be like now if I hadn't found you-lacking ambition, lacking the joy in the lighter pleasures of the world, lacking any fascination with the magic of gold and endowed at the same time with very moderate intellectual and no material means whatever- I would just have strayed miserably about and gone into a decline. You give me not only aim and direction, but so much happiness as well that I cannot be dissatisfied with the otherwise rather wretched present; you give me hope and certainty of success. I knew it before you loved me and I know now that you do love me and it is your doing that I have become a self-confident, courageous man.

Marty, my sweet treasure, our happiness rests finally in our love, I don't want any more than you want for us both, not out of cowardice but because I am aware of the insignificance of other desires compared with the fact that you are mine . And you are so sweet and so good. The only news I have, my darling, is that Schonberg comes to see me every day, that I am fairly satisfied with his condition, but that as soon as his brother Alois is back I am going to pursue the project of his Italian journey. Mother was in bed with a temperature yesterday, a minor recurrence of her old protracted lung trouble; today her temperature is normal again, but it means that I have to go home every day. Pauli is not well, either. Yesterday I went on an excursion with Dolfi to Pötzleinsdorf; she waited for me while I was seeing my patient, and then we walked back via Dornbach. She is the sweetest and best of my sisters, has such a great capacity for deep feeling and alas an all-too-fine sensitiveness be a most affectionate friend to you; her instinct allows her always be a most affectionate friend to you; her instinct allows her to guess what her judgment cannot provide.

Is it possible, Marty, that your wish about which I have been racking my brains for so long, is nothing more than a loofah? Surely you must want something else and will let me know, It is always worth sending you something simply for the pleasure you take in it, even if the object isn't worth it....But you always see the intention behind it, don't you?

My sweet darling, I meant to write more today, but Schönberg and Franceschini have been here all the afternoon, then we had write to you instead of being allowed to kiss your sweet lips.

So let us part for today with a fond goodnight.

In devoted love
Your
Sigmund

19
To Martha Bernays

Vienna, Sunday
September 16, 1883

My sweet little woman

I also want to ask for something: that you accept from me, as atonement for some mean thoughts and some criticism which did not do you justice, the two things you have wished for. I will get the little dictionary, and you must let me know what the jacket is going to cost. If I cannot afford it now, I want to be allowed to do it later, next month. But don't deny yourself, my precious, any little luxury; I don't. And you are so young and can be so pleased with things, and I l know that everyone who sees you" wants to give you some pleasure, so why shouldn't I be allowed to do the same? Your letter moves me like the voice of an angel, and helps me to rise above all my silly worries about you and above my deeply shattered emotional condition. I did not want to talk about it on our monthly memorial day, but I cannot conceal it from you any longer: I have just returned from the funeral of my friend Nathan Weiss.

On the thirteenth, at 2 P.M., he hanged himself in a public bath in the Landstrasse. He had been married hardly a month and had returned ten days ago from his honeymoon. He left two letters, one to the police asking them to inform his parents tactfully and to suppress any word of it in the newspapers, the other to his wife. By Thursday evening the news was already known in the hospital, a colleague rushed to his apartment to take him to the hospital in order to scotch the rumor; but the door was locked. His brother, *Sekundararzt* in die hospital, confirmed the news. Early on Friday morning Lustgarten2 came to see me while I was still in bed, soon afterwards two other colleagues, all with the same news, but we just could not believe it, it was too difficult to conceive of a man who combined in himself more restlessness and zest for life than we had seen in anyone else, as dead and silent. Even now, though l have just heard the thud of the earthen his coffin, I cannot, get used to the thought.

And why did he do it? He was well on the way to achieving everything he had been striving for, he had become a Dozent, enjoyed a considerable reputation in his field; since directing a department in the hospital he was assured of a large practice, he had just succeeded in getting married-but that was the trouble; the details that drove him to his death are unknown doubt, but that they are linked up with his marriage is beyond doubt. I have for gotten how much I have told you of what preceded this marriage, but I think I had better repeat here all I know about him, for his death was by no means an accident, rather it was 'a logical outcome of his temperament; his good and bad qualities had combined to bring about his downfall; his life was as though Composed by a writer of fiction, and this catastrophe the inevitable end.

His father is lecturer at the religious college of Vienna, a very brilliant scholar who, had he chosen to study Chinese instead of rabbinical law, would certainly have become a university professor; despite all this, however, he is a very hard, had, brutal man" My father's a monster," Nathan used to say. His mother is a decent, simple, good-natured woman, who bore many children and shared all the vicissitudes of life with her husband, although their life lacked any deeper relationship. In that home there was no love and bitter poverty, no education and endless demands. To satisfy the fathers colossal vanity, all the sons had to study, most of them did not get very far, went to the dogs; six months ago one of them shot himself because he could see no other way out. Only Nathan and one brother, now working in the hospital, got anywhere. Nathan was the most gifted, he inherited all his father's talent, but he was a good fellow. He was not often looked upon as such; it was always said that he had a bad character and many of his actions confirmed it. This was due, I think, to his main driving force- self-love; I might almost say self-adulation. No doubt he was superbly equipped to get on in the world, and so long as things were difficult for him he never bothered about what means to choose. He was incapable of any self-criticism, over looked, forgot, and forgave himself anything he had done badly or which showed him up in a bad light; on the other hand, anything that raised his 'self- importance he cultivated and exhibited in front of others. Breuer said rightly that he reminded him of the story of the old Jew who asks his son; "My son, what do you want to be?" And the son answers: "Vitriol, the stuff that eats its way through everything." Weiss really was vitriol and he really did eat his way through everything. His gigantic self-importance was matched by an energy of an unusual kind, an ability to burrow his Way into things and never let go. But I don't think he owed his success to this ability; I always saw him in another' light. I Considered his extraordinary appetite for life to be the outstanding quality in his character.

He took pleasure in his own speech, in his own thoughts, yes, even insignificant, indifferent actions of everyday life, and was convinced that no one could perform them as well as he. Every- thing he said and thought possessed plasticity, a warmth, a quality of importance, which was meant to conceal the lack of deeper substance. For his gifts were not remarkable, he knew little, never the basic conditions delved very deep and he lacked completely the basic conditions for scientific work: criticism and thoroughness. As a result his achievements are of moderate value, and lack any original content. It was his temperament his personality, the liveliness and clarity of his presentation, which brought about meadows, forest, sunshine, but how differently they express it! When Weiss talked of a well-known phenomenon he gave the impression of a great discovery freshly made by him; when he addressed one in his strange, witty gibberish as "a compromised central European," one really did feel compromised; one could as little help believing in his assertions as one can help laughing when someone else laughs, or yawning A when someone else yawns. Much of the high opinion in which people held his ability was inspired by himself, for he was always on the spot buttonholed everyone, talked only about himself and of himself as the most able expert on the subject with which he just happened to be occupied. Another positive element in his talent was the quickness with which he thought and his brilliance at put- ting two and two together. One could almost say that his self-confidence was the direct physiological result of the vivacity, quickness, and clarity of his thought processes. He behaved invariably as we would after a lot of champagne: light, capable, and happy. With his incessant restlessness, he gave the impression of a raving maniac. For this reason it is so difficult for any of us to imagine him dead; not for a minute had anyone ever seen him quiet.

He was always concentrated, always preoccupied with the same, and as a result was so one-sided that he lacked not only interest for any science outside a certain field of medicine but also the ability to enjoy human and natural things. For fourteen years he hardly ever left the hospital, whirled like a fast-moving automaton out of the building and into the restaurant, into the coffee- house, and back. His recreation consisted of playing cards and chess, at which he was a master, and in spite of the agitation it produced in him and which sometimes caused him to be exceedingly ruthless, it was a pleasure comparable to a theater performance to watch him at play and to listen to his original, biting Wit. Even when he was well able to afford it, he could not be induced to travel and see something of the world. On his return from his honeymoon he said to me; "I'm not one of those people who can stare for hours into a lake and enthuse about it."-He avoided any kind of social life that might require him to make an effort, he didn't look at anything and didn't know what was going on in the world. As a result he was completely lacking in manners, and cynical, and when you and Minna saw him and found him odd enough, it was when he happened to be on his most civilized and decent behavior. Once, while still a student, he fell in love with a girl who didn't like him and who took another man who had everything he lacked. Since then no affection has softened his nature.

He paid for his success partly at the cost of his reputation, and had few friends, although for quite some time people had given up passing judgment on him and had accepted him as a phenomenon not subject to the usual laws. He was incapable of friendship and could talk to a man for years without once asking what he did, but he was very communicative and whoever he happened to see most often was the person in whom he confided most. His life seemed to be an open book; only after his death did we discover that he concealed a lot. For me he had more friendship based on respect than for many others, and he had grown fond of me. He talked of being permanently at my disposal, and   the event of his death of making me his heir. All this took place at a time when his ambition, mitigated by his inborn good nature, was directed at fairly noble aims. As soon as he didn't need them any more he abandoned his mean ways, his real achievements lessened the appearance of his presumptuousness, the recognition' given him for his abilities made the buying of it superfluous. Then came the moment when he wanted to appear as a noble, unselfish human being, to achieve for his character what he had achieved for his ability. Hence his generosity towards me, hence the long list of good intentions which drove. him to his death. Influenced perhaps by the happiness of lovers around him, he tried to create the same thing for himself, tried and tried and allowed himself no time to let it come his way. Whenever a colleague produced a fiancée, he would inquire about the latter's sister, but always came too late. He got himself introduced to the houses of a few wealthy people, but whether he didn't play there the role he aspired to, or whether by chance he just didn't find anyone he declared in any case that he was going to marry a poor girl He wanted to make a girl happy, and impress the world. On his list he had three possibilities, Helene F., the young Hammerschlag girl and- our Rosa, whom he may have seen once. (I learned this only yesterday.) He started on the conquest of the first probably because he did not look askance at taking in a little wealth on the side I Well remember the day, three years ago, when he said to me: "A woman came for a consultation today with her 'two daughters. Charming people; if I had the money and weren't ill [at that time he thought he was], I'd marry the elder girl at once." It was she who later became his wife, although he did not see her for some time. Finally he introduced himself to the family and began to court the girl. The family accepted him from the beginning, but for a long time the girl resisted him. He seems to have encountered a real Brünnhilde, a reserved, not very yielding, extremely demanding creature. She was considered intelligent and sensible. I saw two letters from her W g the impression of sound, sober respectability, but little feminine refinement in handwriting or expression. She was twenty-six, had turned down many good offers of marriage and didn't seem to feel any need for love. He now courted her ardently, and met with nothing but criticism and rebuff. She told him he was arrogant, mannerless, had a thousand- faults which he would have to get rid of; he listened to every word, promised to improve, became gentle, refrained from using abusive language, so that one could actually introduce him to girls. At last she began to give in, thought she loved him, perhaps she had actually begun to feel some affection for him; she couldn't be certain. After all, no girl in love for the first time knows whether or not it is the real thing. He filled the world with the news of his happiness; when asked about the dowry he always answered that he was not worrying about that. Gradually, however, his mood changed, he grew depressed, and finally confidential. There had been differences of opinion between them-he omitted to mention the reasons-and now the girl was melancholic, she wept, wouldn't speak, took' no pleasure in his company. He also divulged that all the sisters were hysterical. I tried to comfort him, told him the girl was evidently sensitive and conscientious, and realized that her affection for him was not strong enough in view of the imminence of the wedding. It couldn't be otherwise, I said, after so short an acquaintance; he ought to give her time and not press her too much. But now he Was determined to win her, he wooed her more time and more ardently, spent about a thousand gulden on presents for her, contributed another huge sum toward her trousseau, converted all his savings into cash so as to furnish their apartment magnificently and made it well-nigh impossible for her to refuse him-and things went from bad to worse.

When he told me that she had asked him to marry her sister instead, and that she was temporarily relieved when the wedding was postponed., I was convinced she did not like him. And I told Breuer about it. He said that if a girl entered marriage in this spirit the greatest misfortune could occur, and that such conditions usually end by someone in the family turning up and declaring: "I will not allow you to marry "-This person, however, did not turn up the entire family urged the poor girl on. She was sent off on a short trip, but returned unchanged. Now I implored him to accept' the fact that she did not love him and to take a trip himself, that on his return he would feel more detached, that the girl would have clarified her mind, and that then he could come to some definite decision. But he just could not bear the thought that a girl could refuse him, and he sacrificed everything recklessly with the single object of not having to face the world as a failure. Her 'family then brought so much stupid pressure upon the girl that she, who could not find the courage for a definite refusal, renounced the postponement. Five days after he had promised me to go on a trip, the Wedding took place. She is supposed to have said: "It's a question of now or never." It is not difficult to guess why she had hesitated. I think he dropped his self-restraint too early, 'and physical aversion and moral disapproval quickly stifled all affection in the still cool and prudish girl. He on the other hand had believed that he could force love as he had forced all his other successes, and a false shame prevented him from letting the World know that he had been rejected.

I saw him once after the honeymoon; he was not alone and couldn't speak freely. Paneth saw him as late as the twelfth, and when asked about his marriage, he said he had known better things, accused himself of being a wretched failure," but again someone was present who prevented any further Confidences. He wasn't Seen anywhere; on the other hand no one wanted to disturb the young couple; all one knew was that her family were continuously in and out of the house. On the thirteenth he hanged himself. What drove him to it?

As an explanation the world is ready to hurl the most ghastly accusations at the unfortunate widow. I don't believe in them. I believe that the realization of an enormous failure, the rage caused by rejected passion, the fury at having sacrificed his whole scientific career, his entire fortune, for a domestic disaster, perhaps also the annoyance at having been done out of the promised dowry, as well as the inability to face the world and confess it all- I believe that all this, following a number of scenes which opened his eyes to his situation, may have brought the madly vain man (who in any case was given to serious emotional upheavals) to the brink of despair. He died from the sum total of his qualities, his pathological self-love coupled with the claims he made for the higher things of life.

Over his corpse began the feud of the families and on his still open grave there sounded a loud discordant scream for revenge, as unfair and as reckless as if he had uttered it himself. The lecturer Friedmann, a relation and colleague of his old father, began "Thy name was Noah, and thy parents associate with it the dictum:"Thou shalt be the comfort and the support of our old Age.' And all this comfort now lies here. And it is written : If a corpse be found, and one does not know by whose hand he died, then one must turn to the next of kin; they are the murderers.' But we, his parents and brothers have not shed his blood- And now in clear words he began to accuse the other family of having dealt the fatal blow. And all this he spoke with the power full voice of the fanatic, with the ardor of the savage, merciless Jew.

We were all petrified with horror and shame in the presence of the Christians who were among us. It seemed as though we have given them reason to believe that we worship the

God of Revenge, not the God of Love. Pfungen's thin voice was lost in the reverberation of the wild accusation of the Jew.

Both his widow and his father have issued special mourning announcements. The papers print two interpretations, both false, one from her family, the other from his. I am afraid there are some ugly revelations still in store for us.

Thus his death was like his life, cut to a pattern: he all but screams for the novelist to preserve him for human memory.

Well, lucky the man who is tied to life by a sweet darling, I just cannot write any more today, Marty.

With fondest Love
Your
Sigmund

20

To Martha Bernays

Vienna, Saturday
October 6, 1883

My dearest treasure

Now you are going to laugh at me: for the first time in ages I don't know what to write to you. I am so engrossed in the reading of papers, medical papers of course, and the trying out of methods, that I felt inclined to begin this letter: "Today's mail due from Wandsbek has not arrived." And besides, I love you so immensely since receiving your last letter that I am sitting here alone and that you are not with me.

Today was a quite working day; I had to skip the morning rounds because I was at the Journal till 9 o'clock. Then I fever-now I have one left for tomorrow which I shall certainly dispose of, too. Tomorrow is Sunday; fortunately I will be on duty; what else can one do on a Sunday when the only person on whose presence one would like to rest is inaccessible? Patience. If I remain as fit and healthy as I am at the moment, something good must come my way. But you are quite, quite right, never again will I interrupt work in your absence.

And you, what are you look like, how, what, I want to know everything about you, and best of all I would like to hear everything all over again every day. My den is getting quite cozy. It's a pity I cannot name a spot where you have sat. But even if there were such a place, it would be covered with periodicals. I am reading my way into medicine. My first contributions were printed today, unsigned of course. The deeper I penetrate into medicine, the more difficult writing for publication becomes Not because I have to fulfil demands that are greater than they used to be. No, because most publications require so much self-denial. If authors had more self-criticism, nine-tenths of them would not be authors. I have to read a great deal of indifferent and even more inaccurate stuff, and cannot of course write like this myself. In medicine a greater part of one's intelligence is spent discarding useless thing; however, this is an inconspicuous way of being intelligent. Anyhow I hope that a deeper absorption in the subject matter will give me the desire and ability to produce something useful.

Marty, does it annoy you to hear me talk about such thing? Oh, you won't be annoyed, you are so good and- between ourselves you write so intelligently and to the point that I am just a little afraid of you. I think it all goes to show once more how quickly women outdistance men. Well, I am not going to lose anything women outdistance men. Well, I am not going to lose anything by it.

Farewell, my girl,
With many affectionate greetings from

Your
Sigmund

21
To Martha Bernays

Vienna, Tuesday
October 9, 1883

My beloved Marty

What I am doing now? I am more industrious than even and feel better than ever. Most of the time I work my way through a mountain of papers, reading partly for myself, partly for the Medical weekly; I sit in the laboratory, where my Method is actually working and looks very fine, although several things still need correcting, and form early in the morning till wards o'clock (I had almost forgotten to tell you) I function in the wards as a *Sekundararzt,* busy learning writing, and occasionally acting as surgeon. The whole situation, my darling, has something heavy about it, akin to a dream or delirium; these are the right conditions to help one survive a long separation; whether they are pleasant it is hard to say; personal feelings don't get much chance of a hearing. Continually having so much to do acts as a kind of narcotic, but as you know I have lately been looking for something to rescue me from my great emotional and excitable state. Now I have it. It seems as though the waves of the great world do not lap against my door; at other times I have to fight against the sensation of being a monk in his cell, as described by Scheffel. Strange creatures are billeted in my brain. Cases, theories, diagnostics, formulas have moved into brain accommodations most of which have been standing empty, the whole of medicine is becoming familiar and fluid to me, here bacteria live, sometimes turning green, sometimes blue, there come the remedies for cholera, all of which make good reading but are probably useless. Loudest of all is the cry: tuberculosis! Is it contagious? Is it acquired? What does it come from? Is Master Koch of Berlin right in saying that he has discovered the bacillus responsible for it?

When a letter from you arrives the whole dream fades, life enters my cell. Then all the strange problems creep away, the mysterious pictures of diseases fade, and gone are the empty theories "according to the present status of science," as they are invariably called.

Then the world turns so warm, so gay, so easy to understand. My sweet darling is no illusion, she does not have to be proved by chemical tests; in fact she can, although no giant, be seen by the naked eye. Fortunately she has nothing, to do with diseases- I hope she is very well- except that she was incautious enough to take a doctor for love. Oh Marty, it is so much more lovely to be a human being than a warehouse for certain monotonous experiences. But one is not allowed to be a human being for an hour unless one has been a machine or a warehouse for eleven hours. And there we are, back where we began.

I hope to hear from you tomorrow, my precious girls. Farewell, try to be a little gay.

Your devoted
Sigmund

22
To Martha Bernays

Vienna, Tuesday, 7 PM
October 15, 1883

My beloved Marty

Your sweet letter of congratulation found me at the journal speculating on how to pin down and improve the Method. Probably the whole of next week will be spent on further experiments after careful preparation. Today I am going to show Breuer the specimens during consulting hours I have no doubt that I have got the thing although just recently it has been behaving rather capriciously. However, behind such whims of nature there usually lurks a chance of learning more. I am thinking of changing my working hours by taking a course with Ultzmann from eleven to twelve instead of the one with Urbantschitsch from four to five, thus leaving the afternoon free for my own work. Also for the pupil, if only she would come, for I already see with horror the day approaching when, etc.

Today is the sixteenth monthly memorial of our engagement and an especially greeting is due to the sweet girl whose letters have continually grown better and cleverer and nobler, although she herself has always possessed these qualities.

Darling Martha, until now we have been in the ascent, haven't we? And have more and more reason to be pleased with each other, which is why we can look forward confidently to the following month; it was only a month ago that I had to complain, but today this seem almost forgotten.

What my work, for which you so sweetly wish me luck, consists of, I cannot tell you without a terribly long explanation. One thing, however, I can divulge: it has to do with a method for the chemical treatment of the brain. Clear? No.

Well, "as is well known," the brain must first of all be hardened (in spirits, for instance) and then finely sliced in order to show where the fibers and cells lie in relation to one another, where fibers lead to, etc. The fibers are the leading ducts of the different parts of the body, the cells are in control of them, so respect is due to these creatures. Now, on the sliced segment of the hardened brain very little is visible, but more appears when they are colored with carmine, because then the cells and flbers grow redder than the other less important parts. Even so, it is still very difficult to see all the fine flbers or even to get very clear pictures. It is well known that silvering and gilding produce beautiful pictures on other specimens-that is, quite different coloring for the different element; now this is also being tried out on the brain. I believe that so far I have succeeded best. These are technical tricks which exist in every craft, but which science cannot do without. Is my darling princess satisfied now?

Such dirty notepaper and such an enormous envelope, she will think, but this is life at the Journal. Fortunately it is just 9A.M. about to be relieved.

Farewell, princess, and I hope I shall often be able to give you good news.

Your
Sigmund

23
To Martha Bernays

At the Journal, Tuesday
October 23, 1883

My beloved Marty

I dare to say "my beloved" although I do occasionally   have had thoughts and write so angrily. If I have offered you again, please put it down on the list with the others and think of my longing, my loneliness, my impatient struggle and shackles that are imposed upon me. Now and again I have something like attacks of despondency and faintheartedness which you, my dear and kind one, must not share. At this time you must laugh at me unclouded judgment. This afternoon, girl, I once more had more had good results, found a new gold method which promises to be capricious, I can never- the less foresee the final result: I shall discover complete or almost completely what I am looking for.

These difficult times will not discourage me so long as we remain healthy and are spared exceptional misfortune. Then we are certain to achieve what we are striving for- a little home into which sorrow may find its way, but never privation, a being-other throughout all the vicissitudes of life, a quite contentment that will prevent us from even having to ask what is the point of living . I know after all how sweet you are, how you can turn a house into a paradise, how you will share in my interests, how gay yet painstaking you how you will be. I will let you rule the house as much as you wish, and you will reward me with your sweet love and by rising above all those weaknesses for which women are so often despised. As far as my activities allow we shall read together what we want to learn, and I will initiate you into things which could not interest a girl so long as is unfamiliar with her future companion and his occupation, All that has happened and is happening will, by the intention you take in it, become an added interest for me. You will not judge me according to the success I do or do not achieve, but according to my intention and my honesty; you will not regret having sacrificed the beautiful years of your youth to fidelity, and I shall be proud of you. You will be able to read me like an open book, it shall be make us so happy to understand and support each other. You will prevent me from doing anything petty, from anger, envy, and the desire for unimportant things, and if you worry about having interfered with my scientific career I will laugh and tell you the story of Benedikt Stilling, a doctor who died a few year ago in Cassel, practiced science in the youth and was then compelled to take a job as a doctor. But for thirteen years he worked every morning on the human spinal cord, the result of which was a great work, and every evening he continued to work on the brain, and he is known as the foremost among the scientists to whom we owe the knowledge of this noble organ. All this shows the industry, the tenacious enthusiasm of Jew, not even coupled with the talent normally expected from Jews. This we can also do.

My beloved Martha, part of what you will be to me you are already. But I expect you to become more and more. Others keep going only under fortunate circumstances, we Marty and I will do the same, although separated and not at all fortunate.

Goodnight, my dearest little women, keep pouring out your heart to me; I feel so sad when you haven't done so for some time.

Your
Sigmund

24

To Martha Bernays

Vienna, Tuesday evening
October 25, 1883

My darling girl

Yes, it is true, we have made a discovery which may not be insignificant, and you must forgive me if I talk a lot about it today. Yesterday in my joy I went to see Breuer as late as 9: 30, and on my way that I thought up all kinds of compliments for his wife, so that she should not be bored by our conversation. For instance, "Not only women are beautiful, chemical preparations can be, too!" and a second one which I actually managed to make use of, as you will learn. Finding no one at home, I settled down in the consulting room and picked up the nearest book-I looked in vain for the cigar box. (I have been granted these rights once and for all.)

The book I picked up I liked so much I decided to sent it to my Martha. Poor sweet princess, it is already ordered for you, but just now when I would so much like to give it to you as a celebration of our success. I am quite poor. As things never work out as one expects them to, Frau Mathilde came home first and informed me that I wouldn't be able to see her husband until eleven o' clock, that he actually was downstairs on his way to fetch the children, who had gone to the Karl Theater, where the Meininger are now giving a special performance. She hoped I wasn't annoyed. I was not in the least annoyed. I just mentioned that I had had such a pleasant day I would like to end it in the best possible company(my second compliment, which actually earned me a handshake.), and then ran downstairs, where I met Breuer. "Let's go for a walk," he said. We went arm toward the Karl Theater and when I broke my news and talked of it for a long time and finally asked his forgiveness for holding forth on a subject which might not interest him, he good enough to say: "Few things interest me more."

This afternoon at three I went to see Fleischl, whom I found again in a miserable state; I showed him the preparations one after the other: first the silver and then the gold made with the unreliable method, then new ones. While I was in the midst of the first gold preparation, Brücke arrived. "Anything to be seen?""Yes, brain gildings." " Ah, that's very interesting, especially since gold has the reputation of not being much use for this." " But this is a new method, Herr Hofrat." "I see, your methods alone will make you famous yet." And with that he went off. Fleischl was quite beside himself with delight. Sanguine as he is, he congratulated me over and over again and advised me to concentrate for the next seven year on the exploitation of this discovery. I laughed out loud and told him I would starve long before then. "You won't starve," he said. Then he confided in me that he too had a discovery up his sleeve: to build a new kind of accumulator for electricity; if it came off he would make a lot of money and give me enough to allow me to concentrate on this work without any worries. Needless to say, this suggestion cannot be taken seriously, but it is rather significant of the warmth of our relationship nowadays. I thanked him accordingly and asked him, in the event of his discovery succeeding, to give me just enough to travel to Hamburg in the summer. This was granted. Then I asked him if he would use the same method for an examination, say of the retina, that fine sensitive little skin at the back of the eye, which is actually part of the brain, and to my great joy he promised to start on it as soon as the exhibition had closed. To my joy because to teach an old teacher something is a pure, unmitigated satisfaction.

Then I went to Breuer, whom I found rather cantankerous after his luncheon: his microscope was not quite in order. As a result I wasn't able to show him everything, but what he did see drew from him quite a number of admiring comments. Then he said:"Now that you have the weapon, I wish you a happy war." No doubt it will mean a great deal of work before the first paper can appear of which my little women will receive an offprint. The great question is: Will this method also be suitable for tracing the fine nerve fibers in the tissues, in the skin in the glands, etc? If this is the case, then indeed a new prospect will be opened. My material situation would no doubt also profit from it; the year of waiting for my darling would be shortened. Should it not come off so well, sure it won't fail; I gave it another test today. What I am afraid of is that I may succeed with new methods, which would entail so much work that my head would spin with the commotion.

Apart from its practical importance, this discovery has an emotional significance for me as well I have succeeded in doing something I have been trying to do over and over again for many years. When I survey the time since I first began to tackle this problem, I realize that my life has progressed .I have longed so often for a sweet girl who might be everything to me, and now I have her. The same men whom I have admired from afar as inaccessible, I now meet on equal terms and they show me their friendship. I have remained in good health and done nothing dishonorable; even to me have become available, and I feel safe from the worst fate, that things that are still missing and to have my Marty, now so fate away and lonely as her letter shows, close by me, have her all to myself, and in her tender embrace look forward to the further development of our life.

You have shared my sadness; now today share with me my joy, beloved, and don't get the idea that there is even anything in the center of my thoughts but you.

With affectionate greetings and kisses
Your
Sigmund

25
To Martha Bernays

Vienna, Thursday, 5 P.M
November 15, 1883

My sweet princess

This is to be your name from now on. I have been thinking of you more than usual during these past days, and just want to remind you- by wishing myself luck and success for the return of the date which gave you me- of the special coincidence that this is the seventeenth monthly memorial and that the seventeenth is again a Saturday. But I won't have to renew my courtship, will I? Today is a holiday and I have done no work whatsoever, in order to refresh myself. The weather is quite horrible; this evening I think I will go and see Hammerschlag. I am so weary that it will do me good if some is friendly to me . What's more, than will ask after you I will have a chance to talk about you.

What you said in your last letter about Mill and his wife should have inspired me on the spot to tell you something about them both. The essay by Brandes gives only a personal impression of the man, it is far from being an evaluation of his whole position in our contemporary history. I got the idea of reading him when Gomperz entrusted to me the translation of his last work. At the time I found fault with his lifeless style and the fact that in his work one could never find a sentence or a phrase that would remain in one's memory. But later on I read a philosophical work of his which was witty, epigrammatically apt, and lively. Very possible he was the man of the century most capable of freeing himself from the domination of the usual prejudices. As a result- and this always goes hand in hand – he lacked the sense of the absurd, on several points, for instance in the emancipation of women and the question of women altogether. I remember that a main argument in the pamphlet I translated was that the married women can earn as much as the husband. I dare say we agree that housekeeping and the care and education of children claim the whole person and practically rule out any profession; even if simplified conditions relieve the women of housekeeping, dusting, cleaning, cooking, etc. All this he simply forgot, just as he omitted all relations connected with sex. This is altogether a topic on which one does not find Mill quite human. His autobiography is so prudish or so un-earthy that one would never learn from it that humanity is divided between men and women, and that this difference is the most important one. His relationship to his own wife strikes one as inhuman, too. He marries her late in life, has no children from her, the question of love as we know it is never mentioned. Whether she was the wonderful person he revered is generally doubted. In all his writings it never appears that the women is different from the man, which is not to say she is something less, if anything the opposite. For example he finds an analogy for the oppression of women in that of the Negro. Any girl, even without a vote and legal rights, whose hand is kissed by a man willing to risk his all for her love, could have put him right on this.

It seems a completely unrealistic notion to sent women into the struggle for existence in the same way as men. Am I to think of my delicate, sweet girl as a competitor? After all, the encounter could only end by my telling her, as I did seventeen months ago, that I love her, and that I will make every effort to get her out of the competitive role into the quite, undisturbed activity of my home. It is possible that a different education could suppress all women's delicate qualities- which are so much in need of protection and yet so powerful- with the result that they could earn their living like men. It is also possible that in this case it would not be justifiable to deplore the disappearance of the most lovely thing the world has to offer us: our ideal of womanhood. But I believe that all reforming activity, legislation and education, will founder on the fact that long before the age at which a profession can be established in our society, nature will have appointed woman by her beauty, charm and goodness, to do something else.

No, in this respect I adhere to the old ways, to my longing for my Martha as she is, and she herself will not want it different; legislation and custom have to grant to woman many rights kept from them, but the position of woman cannot be other what it is to be an adored sweetheart in youth, and a beloved wife in maturity.

There is so much more to say on this subject, but I think we see eye to eye anyway. Farewell, my sweet girl. Your letter won't come today, so I will go out.

Affectionate greetings and kisses
From your
Sigmund

26

To Martha Bernays

Hotel Stadt Freiberg, Leipzig, 7:30 PM.
December 16, 1883

My sweet princess

Isn't this absurd? I have just been laughing out loud Isn't it amazing that I am suddenly writing to you under a printed letter- head and smoking a ten-pfennig cigar tasting of straw? And that I have only six kreutzer in my pocket! Instead of the usual Austrian money I have silver and gold marks whose value impresses me so little that I would be tempted to spend the whole lot today if it weren't so dark that I daren't go out. I am going to write to you now with as much leisure and peace as I wrote last in a hurry, for it is only 7:45 and I have four hours to myself before meeting my brother;1 by then I should normally feel sleepy, but who could sleep under such strange circumstances? Marty, you will already have observed that at heart I am still a child; I can be so happy simply because I am in another place, have different money in my pocket, because bread here is free, and because my windows look out on Halle'sche Strasse instead of on Courtyard III2. Laugh if you like, I intend to remain like this as long as possible and then one day we shall laugh together under similar conditions. On the other hand, there is one thing I 'must try .not to think about, and that is our almost certainly thwarted reunion; otherwise-but you were right in your letter, my darling. I will miss your letters of tomorrow and the day after, very much.

I must say I do find traveling third class at night pretty unpleasant. The human being whose astronomical geography is in his blood and nerves, being to feel sleepy at a certain hour and is dissatisfied when he finds nothing prepared for it. The morning was cold and gray and drizzly, fit only for ducks. Not till we reached Saxony did the sky begin to clear and it turned quite nice in the afternoon. I did not pay much attention to Saxon Switzerland because I know it so well from my wandering on foot; I preferred to read the book by Dr. Luther. But I took a good look at the Elbe and if you arrive in Hamburg in time its waters will whisper many thousand greetings. Between Dresden and Riesa I had my first great adventure, unpleasant at the time, pleasant in retrospect. You know how I am always longing for fresh air and always anxious to open windows, above all in trains. So I opened a window now and stuck my head out to get a breath of air. Whereupon there were shouts to shut it (it was the windy side), especially from one particular man. I declared my willingness to close the window provided another, opposite, were opened, it was the only open window in the whole long carriage. While the discussion ensued and the man said he was prepared to open the ventilation slit in- stead of the window, there came a shout from the background: "He's a dirty Jew!"-And with this the whole situation took on a different color. My first opponent also turned anti-Semitic and declared: "We Christians consider other people, you'd better think less of your precious self," etc.; and muttering abuses befitting his education, my second opponent announced that he was going to climb over the seats to show me, etc. Even a year ago I would have been speechless with agitation, but now I am different; I was not in the least frightened of that mob, asked the one to keep to himself his empty phrases which inspired no respect in me, and the other to step up and take what was coming to him. I was quite prepared to kill him, but he did not step up; I was glad I refrained from joining in the abuse, something one must always leave to the others. With the compromise of ventilation-slit versus Window, Act I came to an end. The conductor summoned by me took neither side but offered to escort me to another compartment, which I declined. I later, when several people opened the windows am order to get out, ready for a fight. The anti-Semite this time with ironic politeness renewed his request. No, said I, I'd do nothing of the kind, told him is turn to the conductor, and I held my own as far as the next station. There the conductor again refused to say anything, but another official, who happened to have heard of the issue but not of the scene, decided that in winter all windows had to be lost-a storm of jeers, abuses, and threats broke out, until I turned round and yelled at the ring leader to come on over and make my acquaintance. I was not at all sure of the outcome. The answer was that no one was talking about me at all, they had no intention of having their conversation interrupted, but--and from then on-everything was quiet. I do think I held my own quite well, and used the means at my disposal courageously; in any case I didn't fall to their level. After all, I am no giant, haven't any hackles to show, no lion's teeth to Hash, no stentorian roar, my appearance is' not even distinguished; all this would have had a lightning effect on that mob, but they must have noticed that I wasn't afraid and I didn't allow this experience to dampen my spirits. So much time and space has been spent on this silly story. Now I must order another sheet of paper.

The journey here from Dresden is endless; it was 5:30 when I arrived and already dark. I hired a porter as a guide first to the post office to see whether Emanuel might possibly have changed his traveling plans; when this was not the case I asked to be taken to a hotel near the Magdeburg station where I had ordered a room with-two beds for him and myself and another room for Mr._Robin-son3." By a strange coincidence it is called the Hotel Stadt Freiberg, the tower where Emanuel and I met for the first time, where I was ' born. (Needless to say, it is not called after the same Freiberg.) There I made myself look a little more human and hurried to the mirror to see 'what I actually looked like. My self-confidence had been somewhat increased by the battle with the infidels, but sank again when I saw myself in the mirror. No, I don't-look at all noble; neither the blackest coat nor the whitest shirt could conceal my obvious plebeianism. But an elegant princess 'loves me nevertheless, and when I have money, which is as good as certain(my self-assurance tells me so) then I shall dress her in the most beautiful clothes and it will never occur to a .soul that she could have married anyone but a prince. Then I made my 'way slowly toward the Magdeburg station and bought myself some cigars; by then, however, it was time to satisfy a gigantic - appetite with a meal which didn't bear much resemblance to my Viennese suppers. There hadn't been time for a proper luncheon. In the Stadt Freiberg restaurant I sat among the Leipzig Philistines, listening to their talk and watching their faces. They talk just as much rot as the people at home, but they look more human; I don't see so many grotesque and animal-like faces, so many deformed skulls   potato "noses here. On the contrary, if I were in Vienna 1 would think I was in the company of men of letters, professors, and architects.' However, not much seems to lie behind these finer, sharper features. But I heartily dislike the Saxons' way of talking about things; they are continually discussing topics which We would never seriously talk about except at rare moments. Those ethical truths with which we are all pretty familiar these fellows pronounce like so many maxims lifted out of an anthology; they spread ideals, as it were, like butter on bread, and yet they are certainly no more deeply influenced by them than our Philistines are.

The room from which I write, beloved, is quite nice, high up, but has only single windows, and judging by the way I feel, my poor Emanuel will be pretty cold. At eleven o'clock however, they are to come and light the stove; this I have arranged. But what if he does not turn up today? In that case I shall have to meet every train tomorrow, and if he still doesn't come, I shall have to pay the whole bill, travel to Dresden and there borrow 'something from Hammerschlag's brother-in-law. Charming prospect! But that he won't Come is out of the question; it is only my habit of preparing myself for every eventuality that makes me think of it. I feel so well and adventurous. But now comes the bitter side. I won't be able to see you, 'my treasure. I have the little ring for you' in my pocket, and long to slip it on your finger myself. It also needs some explanation; because a simple plain gold ring-it turns out to be a little wider than I expected-looks rather like something which one day, to my delight, you will wear, but cannot wear yet. We will have to have it altered; our monogram put on it, for example, covered with enamel. Let   know soon, Marty, if you want me to have this done in Vienna. For you must be able to wear the ring.

Tomorrow I will hardly have time to write more than a card, I have also got to pay a visit to the Altschuls3 in Dresden. So I shall be leaving here tomorrow evening or early Tuesday; Oh, how disgusting it is that I cannot travel farther.

Farewell, my dearest beloved girl, and keep well and be a little gay and take courage and love me

Your most devoted
Sigmund

27
To Martha Bernays

Vienna, Wednesday evening
December 20, 1883

My precious darling,

In today's quiet I can at last tell you more about Dresden; just the pleasantest of my impressions there have not been mentioned. Right next to the castle we discovered a wonderful cathedral, then a theater, and finally a spacious building-square, with a large courtyard and in each corner a tower, built in the style of our Belvedere1-which Philipp2 seriously insisted must be the castle because it was so beautiful. However it was the so-called Zwinger, which houses all of Dresden's museums and art treasures. At last we found the picture gallery where we spent about an' hour, the old boys chiefly to rest themselves, I to bring home with 'me a few fleeting impressions of these famous works of art. I believe I acquired there a lasting benefit, for until now I have always suspected it to be a silent understanding among people who don't have much to do, to' rave about pictures painted by the famous masters. Here I rid myself of this barbaric notion and myself began to ad- mire. 'If here are magnificent things in the Zwinger; some I knew from photographs and reproductions and could point out to the two Englishmen for instance, the painting. by Van Dyck showing the children of the unfortunate Charles I, the later Charles II, James II, and a young, plump little princess. Then I saw the Veronese with the most beautiful heads and bodies, madonnas, martyrs, etc.; I hardly had time to glance at them all. In a small room by itself I discovered what, according to the way it is displayed, must be a gem. Looking closer, I saw it was Holbein's "Madonna" Do you know this picture? Kneeling in front of the Madonna are several ugly women and 'an unattractive little girl, to the left 'a man with a monk's face, holding a boy. The Madonna holds a boy in her arms and gazes down on the worshipers with such a holy expression. I was annoyed by the ordinary ugly human faces, but learned later they were the family portraits of the Mayor of X, who had commissioned the painting. Even the sick misshapen child whom the Madonna holds in her arms is not meant to be the Christ child, rather the wretched son of the Mayor, whom the picture was sup- posed to cure. The Madonna herself is not exactly beautiful—the eyes protrude, the nose is long and narrow-but she is a true queen of heaven such as the pious German mind dreams of. I began to understand something about this Madonna. Now, I happened to know that there was also a Madonna by Raphael there and I found her at last in an equally chapel-like room and a crowd of people in silent devotion in front of her. You are sure to know her, the Sistina. My thoughts as I sat there were: Oh, if only you were with me! The Madonna stands there surrounded by clouds made up of in- numerable little angel heads, a spirited-looking child on her arm, St. Sixtus (or is it the Pope Sixtus?) looking up on-one Side, St. Barbara on the other gazing down on the two lovely little angels who are sitting low down on the edge of the picture: The painting emanates a magic beauty 1- at is inescapable, and yet I have a serious objection to raise against the Madonna herself. Holbein's Madonna is neither a woman nor a girl, her exaltation and sacred humility silence any question concerning her specific designation. Raphael's Madonna, on the other hand, is a girl, say sixteen years old; she gazes out on the world with such a fresh and innocent expression, half against my will she suggested to me a charming, sympathetic nursemaid, not from: the celestial world but from ours. My Viennese friends reject this opinion of mine as heresy and refer to a superb feature round the eyes making her a Madonna; this I must have missed during my brief inspection. But the picture that -really captivated me was the "Maundy Money," by Titian, which of course I' knew already but to which I had never paid any special. attention. This head of Christ, my darling, is the only one that enables even people like ourselves to' imagine that such a person did exist. Indeed, it seemed that I was compelled to believe in the eminence of this man because the figure is so convincingly presented. And nothing divine about it, just a noble human countenance, far from beautiful yet full of seriousness, intensity, profound thought, and de4epp inner passion; if these qualities do not exist in this picture, then there is no such thing as physiognomy. I would love to have gone away with it, but there were too many people about, English Ladies making copies, English ladies Sitting about and Whispering, English ladies wandering about and gazing. So I went away with a full heart.

At three o'clock I accompanied the brothers to the Reichenberg train, drank a farewell glass of Rhine wine with Emanuel, had my luggage taken by porter to the Altstädter station and walked through the whole town and the crowds of shoppers as far as the Bismarckplatz-right beside the station from which I leave-where the Altschuls live. It took a little While before someone appeared; the room in which I sat brought back to me the peculiarities of the family. Then there arrived a delicate, dark girl, not beautiful, but sympathetic and gentle; this was Fraulein Emmy, for Whom I had special greetings. A pleasantly animated conversation was interrupted first by the appearance of little Marie, an even more delicate creature with large gray eyes. Then came the father, a powerfully built man with a gray beard and easygoing manners, then his wife, and then the others. The wife, the third sister whom I now know ld (Frau Hammerschlag, Frau Schwab, and her), not much older than Frau- H., looks quite worn out, did not say much and made a dignified impression. My Viennese friends have assured me that she is a most remarkable woman, and I am quite prepared to believe it. The husband strikes one as a powerful personality; he has lived many years in America, then in England. Almost all the children were born in England; at the moment two sons are in America and the others are thinking of going there, too. The father received me very warmly, insisted on my prolonging me stay (with which my purse did not agree), involved me in a conversation on scientific questions for which he showed a lively and Considerable understanding. He is an ardent freethinker and has brought up all his children outside of the faith. Apart from Emmy, who gives English lessons, there was the younger girl, Clare, who arrived only yesterday from Berlin where she teaches singing, and two boys with the most delicate Jewish faces. I stayed till 11:80, the conversation was easy going, the tone set largely by the stories of the plain and animated girl from Berlin. Someone was sent to fetch the eldest son, who is a junior counselor-at-law, but he couldn't be found. As it was striking eleven and the old man was about to take me next door to tell me about his illness, the young man arrived, accompanied me to the station, and stayed with me till one o'clock. we found; we were of the same age and talked freely together. Every member of the family sent greetings to you. Needless to say, they knew all about you, the Viennese had sent them my dossier, and my engagement to a noble lady from the far north doubt strongly emphasized as one of my peculiarities.

Now, my darling Marty, how about this for a good gossip! I hope I will hear from you again tomorrow. Farewell and keep well for

Your
Sigmund

Most beautiful Marty, don't be Cross, the little ring won't leave till tomorrow.

28
To Martha Bernays

Vienna, Monday
January 7, 1884

My beloved princess

I cannot initiate your innocent mind into the secrets of the hospitals administration as late in the day as this (by the time I have finished this letter the date will no longer be true). Let us have a chat instead, Marty! The daily report says I have been hard at work till 7 P.M., that I then let myself be inveigled into a game of taroc,1 and then again worked a bit, and that I am not even tired. Today I put my case histories in order at last and started. on the study of a nervous case; thus begins a new era! In the evening I meant to examine something through the ophthalmoscope which I had carried off from Meynert's clinic, but realize that I am out of practice, which saddens me. I must practice again. In the evening the newspaper boy brought me for the first time a few lovely off- prints and books, which I shall review and then keep. Even a little piece of material for the Method arrived today. Otherwise the Method is idle, for as yet nothing has hardened; I have managed to find only a very small improvement This is all there is to say about me, and the Princess can see that in my godforsaken boredom I am doing the one thing that is good and wholesome for me now over to you, my darling. I am so glad that for quite a while now there has been no mention in our letters of any "mutual" in Disposition, also that time we have skipped our little monthly squabble which used to appear with such impressive regularity at the end of every first week, so that by the seventeenth2 we both had a chance to forgive each other. Let us hope we have now grown out of this peculiarity. Your suggestion, by the way, that I state things clearly instead of alluding to them, made me laugh. How would it be if we reversed the roles once more? Very amusing, But I am no longer so silly as write you lengthy dissertations now (for which you don't even thank me), if we are not going to meet till July.

I must say I don't find the notion that every girl has a silent admirer who eventually marries her very convincing; I would be less surprised if some girl had from five to 36,000 and that the majority, about whom there is nothing much to admire, had none at all- but it is one nature's more charitable institutions. Almost as wonderful is the institution that every man find a girl who sees in him the perfection of manhood, whereas in reality he is a miserable devil living by the grace of God's patience. But what are we philosophizing about?

Let us not make the world more complicated than it is already, and if one is in love oneself and has a lot to do, one ought to leave such clichés to unemployed novelists. That's what you would say, and you are quite right. As for me. I am glad you have only one suitor and so many thousands, if only because out of so many there might be one who is better than I, and to slay 25,000 rivals (you note that I place you in the first category) would be difficult for me just now, as I am so busy.

Dearest little women, I have been afflicted with a week's duty, but tomorrow I am going to walk ostentatiously out, and- exchange five marks. If you are absolutely broke, you must let me know. If I make a discovery during the next three months you shall have the golden snake which I promised you in Nothnagel's time Fare well my sweet treasure.

Sigmund

29
To Martha Bernays

Vienna at the Journal
Thursday, January 10 1884

My precious darling

Comfort is the last thing I am entitled to, and it is not because you would have taken care of my comfort that I miss you. If you look at the little book we planned to keep as chronicle of our engagement and which, as a result of insufficient participation by one of us, has not been kept up, you will find an entry to the effect that you promised to do all in your power not to leave me. I took this promise as a firm guarantee that you would stay with me. Whether you put up enough resistance when the project of moving arose, whether one person's1 determination was more decisive for you than my wise- all I shall not investigate, and I really would not know how to start the investigation. But you must not say that shouldn't have let you go. How could I demand from you sacrifices that had advantages only for me ? No, that wasn't possible, and perhaps the other solution wasn't possible, either. Now we are separated, my dear Marty, and we must not belittle my work which alone can bring us together again.

Yesterday I met Father in the street, still full of projects, still hoping. I took it upon myself to write to Emanuel and Phillipp urging them to help father out of his present predicament. He doesn't want to do it himself since he considers himself badly treated. So I sat down last night and wrote Emanuel a very sharp letter. Sorry that has to write about such sad things! Earlier I had been to see the Hammerschalgs, where I was very warmly received. The old professor took me aside and charged me with a delicate mission concerning his young son Albert, who is a medical student; then he informed me that a rich man had given him a sum of money for a worthy person in need, that he mentioned my name and he was herewith handing it to me. I am describing the situation to you in all its crudity. The good professor himself, as has often told me, has experienced great poverty in his own youth sees nothing Shameful in accepting support from the rich. Nor actually do I , but I intend to compensate for it by being charitable myself when I can afford it is not the first time the old man has helped me in this way; during my university years he often, and unasked, helped me out of a difficult situation. At first I felt very ashamed, but later, when I saw that Breuer and he agreed in this respect, I accepted the idea of being indebted to good men and those of our faith without the feeling of personal obligation. Thus I was suddenly in the possession of fifty florins and did not conceal from Hammerschlag my intention of spending it on my family. He was very much against this idea, saying that I worked very hard myself and could not at the moment afford to help other people, but I did make it clear to him that I must spend at least half the money in this way. Than the conversation turned on conditions at home, at and I felt no compunction about giving him some idea of the circumstances and pointing out that the girl were in need of earning a little money. I then asked his permission to bring Rosa up to see them, and after joining the others he started talking about my sister in a way that made me realize that he had arranged beforehand with his wife to question me about them. I don't know any people kinder, more humane further removed from any ignoble motives than they. I hope Rosa will make a friend of Anna Hammerschlag, an admirable girl; perhaps they will recommend her and she will find it easier than I to discuss with Frau H. what can be done about the two other girls. You mustn't forget that Hammerschlags themselves are very poor, have nothing but his pension and what the eldest children earn, the son as a tutor and the girl as a school teacher. The other one, Albert, the medical student, has a large stipend and is an assistant of Ludwing the professor of chemistry. I have always felt more at home this family than with the wealthy Schwabs, quite apart from deep-seated sympathy which. Has existed between myself and the dear old Jewish teacher ever since my school days. Well, now you know everything and I am wondering if you will thank me for my frankness. Knowing you, my one and only girl, I think you will…

I am not entirely dissatisfied with the progress of my work. I work steadily, teach myself and jot down the interesting observations, and then read them up; in any case I am learning a lot, not least about myself. But in time also hope to be able to find some material for publication.

You are right, this is the department where poor Nathan was *Sekundarius*; I am even going to move into the room where he lived for eighteen months and which at night is probably haunted by his ghost. But I sleep well and it will not worry me.

I hope the reading club will be great success; I would love to surprise the ladies at it. Will gentlemen be invited in time? Surely not all the Wolfingen girls are engaged?
" The Chimes". is charming, movingly Beautiful, quite difficult in the beginning. "The Battle of Life" Would be easier and more suitable for all of you. But you know this already in part.

Today I am both at the *Journal* and on duty, which is not so much an accumulation as saving, for one can leave the Journal now and again in order to drop in the department, and this saves a day.

I will write more cheerfully tomorrow, my precious darling, but you must not keep from me the thoughts that cross your mind while reading this latter.
Goodnight.

Your
Sigmund

30

To Martha Bernays

Vienna, Wednesday,
January 16, 1884

My precious Darling

Yesterday was Breuer's birthday; I had hoped to see him at the Club, but he did not turn up and I have just written him a few lines. I had lazy day yesterday; my discovery evaporated in the.

Chemical laboratory, and I was rather annoyed about it. It is hard to find material for publication, and it infuriates me to see how everyone is making straight for the unexploited legacy of nervous diseases.

At the Journal

My precious darling, I realize with horror that I didn't write to you for the seventeenth; the reason is that I have been so caught up in myself, and that I have days on end- they invariably follow one another, it is like a recurring sickness-when my spirits decline for no apparent reason and I tend to get exasperated at the slightest provocation even by the fact that my dear and good sweetheart covers her pages of notepaper, which she sacrifices to me, with such a sprawling hand. It is rather odd, and reminds me of your recent remark that by the time we are sixty-eight, if we ever get that far, we won't be able to boast of much resilience. Even when you use endearments, I don't entirely like it. I think you are misjudging me because we are so far apart and ascribe to me a measure of kindliness, decency and I don't know what, which I have never possessed, never will possess, and which you hardly could have found in me when we were together. When we meet again you may be disappointed on finding that I look different from the lovely picture your tender imagination has painted of me. I don't want you to love me for qualities me, in fact not for any qualities; you must love me as irrationally as other people love, just because I love you, and you don t have to be ashamed of it.

I would rather you didn't make me out so good-natured; I can Hardly contain myself for silent savagery, and your latest letters are so tame; if you weren't such a very sweet angel , I would love to have a good squabble with you. It wasn't so bad, after all, to read something every month that came from the depths of passion. When you are mine we must have a little quarrel at least once a Week, so that your love can always start fresh again. You are probably laughing at all this nonsense, but I am having my bad days, am working a lot but without that real enthusiasm which, according to my calculation, will have returned by the time you read this letter.

I note the calming influence of your gentleness as I Write; in fact I already feel. quite a bit calmer, But it annoys me that I always seem to be talking about myself. I am not really as important to myself as it must appear from my behavior.

As for your cousin. you really shouldn't find it difficult to stand her character. There is, after all, as you have told me yourself, quite a touch of hereditary mental weakness in the family, and what is evident in this girl is a plain simple-mindedness which in it- self explains so many mysterious features in so many people.-By the time you are twenty-six, you too will have to Consider all kinds of furnishings and acquisitions; forgive me for jumping from her to you but this is always how my mind works; whenever I hear of a girl marrying I am first of all interested in her age, and then I work out how many years younger you are Four with luck, four years of work and some success, that ought to do it. But how are you going to survive four years in the quiet of Wandsbek? I just can't stop worrying today. It is no good trying to change things by force..You will be so annoyed with me.

I have copied out the letter I wrote to Breuer; I think it comes off because I felt so strongly, and I am sending it to you because I seem to remember that we intended to write and congratulate him together:

"Dear and admired friend. A year ago I came to your house unaware that it was your birthday and felt then that I was a part of the center of the wide circle to whom you mean so much. One can't always be so lucky This year hoped to shake your hand in the Physiological Club; but on missing you there I was pleased to think that you were able to spend-the evening alone with your wife' and children. My wish for you is that you may keep everything you have and which you 'know so well how to appreciate. I have prevented my Martha from you a present only by pointing out your frequently expressed' dislike for "female needlework." We have nothing else to offer. When I think of my relationship to you and your wife, I find myself most grateful to you for the esteem you have shown me, an esteem which has raised me far above my present station, and by which you either anticipate others or will remain isolated. Neither would be without analogy in your case. In the hope of seeing you again before the end of the month-1 am working more intensely at the moment-Your, Dr. S.F." Rather incoherent, isn't it?

Goodnight, my darling, you may well be a little annoyed, but don't keep it to yourself, better to let go a bit.

**At your faithful
Sigmund**

31
To Martha Bernays

Vienna, Friday evening
January 18, 1884

My sweet girl

I wish I could have any number of days like today, distinguished by small success in work and such affectionate love.

Your letter and your parcel have made me unspeakably happy. My precious Marly, you an; so good and sweet, even when you don't give presents, but you know how to give so charmingly. The buttons I shall always treasure; I am going to put them on at once, although they don't show off to advantage under my high waistcoat. On the other hand, just last week I ordered an open waistcoat —but a moment ago I put them on after all, and they are mag- nificent. The tie produces for me the hitherto unheard-of luxury of a change of ties, for I still possess another decent one. The cigars are excellent; my friend Teych is quite right, they are better than those I used to buy from him and I intend to buy from him in the summer. Schonberg, much as I like him, won't get one, my reason being that he shouldn't smoke. But the truth is: I give nothing away that comes from you.—Incidentally, there is a brief review of his *Hitopedescha* in the evening edition of the *Neue Freie Presse,* well-meaning but polemic and therefore almost certain to have been written by Prof. Miiller. I expect he will send you and Minna a copy.—But the nicest thing of all is your letter, dearer and sweeter than any chocolate, and now, my darling Marty, I am once more your debtor. I should have led a less luxurious life, and saved something for you. I would never have believed that so much money can disappear so fast.

Now as to why I am in good spirits—because your letter made me happy, not just good-humored. Today at last I started working on nervous disorders; I hope I have found the material for my first small clinical publication. For yesterday a poor tailor's ap-prentice arrived with scurvy, the well-known disease in which ecchymosis appears in all organs. Apart from some apathy, he didn't show any visible symptoms. Early this morning he was quite unconscious, which suggested a cerebral hemorrhage. So I went to see nim again before luncheon and found a number of interesting symptoms from which could be deduced the locality of the hemorrhage (always our chief concern in brain disorders). So I sat beside him all the afternoon and observed the interesting and most variable development of the illness till seven o'clock, when symmetrical paralysis appeared, with the result that until his death at 8 P.M. nothing escaped my notice. The publication of this case is justified by several interesting and instructive phenomena, indeed it is imperative, especially if the autopsy tomorrow yields some satisfactory conclusions and confirmation of my diagnosis, which is based on localization. Now I need the *Primarius* consent to publish, which J hope he won't refuse; I intend to keep at him. You see, it is not quite certain yet, nor is it very much, but it is at least a beginning which should make the others take notice of me. It will also bring in a few gulden, perhaps ten—appear possibly in the *Medical Weekly*—*and.* thus by the end of the quarter I hope to be able to contribute a small sum to your spring outfit. Marty, if only I could give you everything I can think of and make you entirely, absolutely my own, how wonderful it would be!

I am not taking Rosa up to the Hammerschlags until Sunday because I understand they won't be home on Saturday. Tomorrow J may go and tell Breuer the good tidings.
With the most affectionate thanks and kisses

From your faithful
Sigmund

Who is again eager to work and to live.(?)

32
To Martha Bernays

Vienna, Monday
January 28, 1884

A moment ago, my beloved treasure, I put the finishing touches to my first clinical publication. There it lies now, eighteen pages long, and it will spread itself in two to three issues. For better or worse I have finished and there is a load off my heart. Now I can tackle something else and my Method will once more have a chance. Fleischl will arrange for the publication in *Brain,* and I still have one to two weeks to work on it, then I give my lecture, show my slides, send off my German and my English manuscripts, and then I am again like "Lucky Hans." Life is hard, but I am drugging myself in work.

Your last letter, my treasure, contained the news I have been looking forward to for a long time. Of course I want your picture, if possible life size, to consecrate my new room into which I still haven't moved, and if I am the only one to receive a picture from you, I shall be especially happy. Otherwise, J really haven't much to say; my cold is still with me, my zest for work has returned, my impatience is greater than ever and one day it will make me explode. I didn't go to Breuer till Saturday, didn't go home for lunch because J was on duty. Schonberg, whom I had invited, waited for me in the coffeehouse till 6:30, as I read on my blackboard. The poor man, our rounds lasted till 7:15 P.M. I now have a compatriot of yours in my department, one Rodewald, who owned an inn in Hamburg, where he himself seems to have been the best customer. He is, moreover, a nervous case and if he hangs on long enough I may write a paper on him, too.

My patient was considerably improved yesterday—but he was only paying me a friendly visit. I still don't have any others.

Look, Marty, do read something good and write to me about it, I am getting such a barbarian with the pressure of my work.

I am not going to accept the job as Meynert's assistant; you wrote very sensibly about it, I probably won't come to Fraulein Fanny Philipp's wedding; I will come only to see my girl, not to make new relations, of whom I have quite enough already.

In my opinion the B on the notepaper is too ostentatious and the M too modest. As you know, I am interested only in the M.

I have got to break off now, my darling; I must go back to the lab. More this evening at the *Journal*.

My precious darling, the *Journal* is always a very pleasant break; I can read a lot, make plans, look into the past and the future. On the other hand, if I do this I usually get annoyed at not being able to carry out my intention of writing to you every day. It was so sweet of you to use that brief stop in Hamburg to send me a postcard. Everything is so sweet of you and about you. Do you think you can continue to love me if things go on like this for years: I buried in work and struggling for elusive success and you lonely and far away? I think you win have to, Marty, and in return I will love you very much. Schonberg told me that Prof. Buhler's wife waited fifteen years for her husband; and now she is older than you will be in fifteen years. Are you prepared to wait fifteen years for me, or would you rather not? In my thoughts I have let you become thirty, and have decided to find you then as young as you were when I met you. No, much younger, for at that time you actually gave quite a matronly impression. But will you really remain as young as that? Don't you feel rather proud of being able to make someone so far away so happy? Well, I can't; with me it all depends on luck, with you just on your temperament. How I am looking forward to your picture!

My work has taken me right into the middle of some quite interesting problems; I discovered by myself all the questions pertaining to the subject, and have arrived at the truth by the method of Herr Kannitverstan. There is a Russian working in the lab who wants to translate my Method. Oh dear, there I go again talking about my stupid work. I am badly in need of an hour's chat with you in order to come out of my shell again. Farewell, my darling. Goodnight.

Your
Sigmund

33
To Martha Bernays

Vienna, Tuesday
January 29, 1884

Dear Fräulein Martha Bernays

At first I could not imagine what the solemn presentation of a red plush visiting card (it is plush, isn't it?) between old lovers like ourselves could mean. I suspected it to contain some kind of picture puzzle, preferably a photograph. Then I got the bright idea that it could be a name card, an idea I found confirmed after reading your letter. Well then, a golden Martha Bernays on a background of red! I like looking at the name, but I know a better one: Frau Martha Freud would strike my eye and my ear as far more beautiful. Your letter, Marty, with its wisdom about love and life, raised my spirits considerably; I have not been so merry and gay for a long time and am so grateful to you. I was very amused to realize how deeply involved you are in being engaged—so deep that you consider all the knights at the Round Table to be engaged without any further proof. If you were not "half married" yourself, you would be just as ready to consider them all unattached. I feel so gay today for no other reason than that produced by your letter, and so much in the mood to hear you talk and to close your mouth every now and again with a lass to make you stop.

Why I never took you to see the Hammerschlags? I often meant to, but sometimes you couldn't and in the end the hours were too precious for me to have shared them with anyone but you. You were not at all awkward at the Breuers'; on the contrary, you were very talkative, more than you were with me at the time; you have no reason to reproach yourself.

Now for my bit of news. I leave here tomorrow; unlike the first room, this one is not associated with memories of sweet happiness. On Tuesday and Thursday two weeks ahead I am going to give my lectures in the Physiological and Psychiatric Clubs. My paper lies before me, finished to the last word. Tomorrow it will be sent off or handed in.

By the end of this week I hope to have finished my paper on the Method in two languages. Nothing new in the department at the moment. I am soon going to choose a topic for a paper from among the problems concerning nervous diseases. I am not worried about failing to find a topic, and I can evidently continue working on this subject on my own. Today the Club met; I sat behind Billroth and Nothnagel and was naughty enough to think: Just wait till you welcome me as you are welcoming the others now! Billroth doesn't know me; Nothnagel, by the way, was rather patronizing last time. Meynert continues to treat me with great respect and advised me to give a lecture at the Medical Society as well, which I don't intend to do just now.

Goodnight, my sweet darling, you do still feel well and still love…

Your
Sigmund

don't you?

34
To Martha Bernays

Vienna, Thursday evening
February 7, 1884

Were I in the position, my Princess, to bestow decorations, you would receive as a reward for your last letter the most beautiful one, that of the White Carrier Pigeon, to be worn on a red ribbon. The letter arrived just as I had started to write my paper and when I had read it I felt so gay that my work went very fast, I had started at 3:30 and by nine I had finished; I leaped for joy— I never miss this exercise if there is the slightest reason for it— and then I meant to write to you. But I was interrupted by a visit—or rather, as a reward to myself I went to the Gasthaus, and so I am writing only today. I was not idle today, either. I copied out the excerpt for the Russian and gave it to him, then I finished the English manuscript and had it corrected by the American, and now I have still got to transcribe the latter and make a few corrections in the German manuscript, and then I am finished with it. Tomorrow I will take them both to Fleischl and then Amen.

I now have time to return once more to my patients and do some reading. I wonder how long it will be before I write something again. Not too long, I hope, A man must get himself talked about.

Silberstein was here again today; he is as devoted to me as ever. We became friends at a time when one doesn't look upon friendship as a sport or an asset, but when one needs a friend with whom to share things. We used to be together literally every hour of the day that was not spent on the school bench. We learned Spanish together, had our own mythology and secret names, which we took from some dialogue of the great Cervantes. Once in our Spanish primer we found a humorous-philosophical conversation between two ilogs which lie peacefully at the door of a hospital, and ap-[Hopriulocl their names; in writing as well as in conversation he was known as Berganza, I as Cipion. How often have I written: *Vttr.riflo Berganza!* and signed myself *Tu fidel Cipio, pero en el **Hospital** de Sevilla!* Together we founded a strange scholarly society, the "Academia Castellana" (AC), compiled a great mass of humorous work which must still exist somewhere among my old papers^ we shared our frugal suppers and were never bored in each other's company. Intellectually he did not like soaring very high; he remained in the human domain; his outlook, his reading, his humor, all were bourgeois and somewhat prosaic. Later when he was ill I became his doctor, and one day he invited all his old colleagues to a farewell party in Hernals, during which he himself with his good-natured expression poured the beer from a barrel in order to conceal his emotion. Then while we were sitting together in a cafe and Rosanes was telling odious jokes, also only, to prevent his sentimentality from overflowing, I was the first to break the ice and in the name of them all made a speech in which I said he was taking with him my own youth, little realizing how true this was. At first I wrote to him off and on; he was badly treated by his half-mad father, of which he complained; I on the other hand tried to arouse his romantic instinct and encouraged him to run away to Bucharest and look for a job more worthy of him; after all, in his youth he had been full of romantic dreams about Red Indians, Cooper's *Leatherstocking,* and sailor's stories. Even quite recently he kept a boat on the Danube, and invited all his friends on trips during which they had to serve as oarsmen and call him Captain. Then you appeared on the *m* -. in and everything that came with you; a new friend, new struggles, new aims. The drifting apart which had gradually developed between us became apparent again when I advised him from Wandsbek against marrying a stupid rich girl whom he had been sent to have a look at. And then we lost contact with each other. He obviously got used to the moneybags, although he is kepi   it's enough as it is; he is prepared to marry this girl so as to establish his independence as a merchant. What has happened to nit', know. And now we have met again and no doubt both of us are thinking how strangely life has treated us, harnessing us both and sending us galloping off, the one in that direction, the other in this.

When he was still very young, Anna was his first love, then he had a liaison with Fanny, in between he was in love with every girl he met, and now he is with none. I was in love with none and am now with one. That is the story of my friend Silberstein, who has become a banker, because he didn't like jurisprudence. Today he is about to gather together again his old boon companions in Hernals, but I am on duty, and in any case my thoughts are not in the past, but elsewhere.

Farewell my beloved treasure, my mailbox was silent today; tomorrow I hope it will speak again to

Your
Sigmund

35
To Martha Bernays

Vienna, Thursday
February 14, 1884

My darling, my girl, my little woman

Do you realize that it is two whole days since I heard from you and that I am beginning to worry! Could you be ill or angry with me? I am only too willing to write to you more often again; best of all I would like to write to you all day long, but what I still prefer is to work all day so as to be able to hold you in my arms for years and years. Otherwise, why should I do so many things now that go against the grain: write papers, give lectures, examine patients, make up to people? But so far in my struggles for recognition I haven't done anything bad and I hope to avoid doing so in the future. Otherwise you wouldn't love me any more. You don't have to worry about this.

I really do wish you had been present to hear my lecture today, Marty. I haven't had such a triumph for a long time. Just imagine your timid lover, confronted by the severe Meynert and an assembly of psychiatrists and several colleagues, trying to draw attention to one of his earlier works, the very one which had been overlooked by Prof. Kupfer. Imagine him beginning with allusions, unable to control his voice, then drawing on the blackboard, in the middle of it all managing to make a joke at which the audience bursts out laughing! The moments in which he is afraid of getting stuck, each time fortunately concealed, become fewer, he slides into the waters of discussion where he sails about for a full hour, then Meynert with some words of praise expresses the assembly's vote of thanks, follows this up with a few appreciative observations, then dissolves the meeting and shakos him by the hand. Then the old gentlemen who hitherto had ignored him congratulate him and gather round him to make a few belated comments, and finally Meynert requests that he make an excerpt for the Society's *Yearbook* and promises to correct the relevant passages with footnotes in his forthcoming book; at last he leaves in an elated mood, wondering whether his work won't after all succeed in making his girl his own. Oh, but now comes the worry about holding one's own, finding something new to make the world sit up and bring not only recognition from the few but also attract the many, the well-paying public.

But I am not going to do anything more today. If there were any justice I should have had a letter from you. Your last, it's true, was again so sweet that anyone less insatiable than I am could go on reading it for ages.

I seriously consider having breakfast in my room so as to save money and at the same time eat better food. Shall I decide on tea or coffee? There are such things as automatic coffee machines, as good as tea machines, and I really don't think there is much to recommend tea, least of all the tea one buys here. What's the opinion of your Highness, my delicate little princess?

Fare thee very well and write again soon to

Your
Sigmund

36
To Martha Bernays

Vienna, Wednesday
March 19, 1884

Her Highness the Princess deigns to look out at me from her plush as if she had guessed again what I did today. Well, I bet she hasn't guessed right. Be prepared for the most unlikely thing you ever heard. In the morning I lay there in the vilest pain and looked at myself in the mirror till I shuddered at the sight of my wild beard. My rage rose and rose until finally it boiled over. I decided not to have sciatica any more, to become human again, and to abandon the luxury of being ill. In no time I was dressed and sitting at the barber's, literally breathed a sigh of relief as I looked once more like a well-trimmed garden hedge, and as the weather was so glorious I walked for a while in the courtyard. It grew more and more easy, after a warm bath I could walk quite well, then I dashed into the laboratory, made up my mind to start work again, in the afternoon played chess in the coffeehouse, and on receiving a brief visit from Prof. Hammerschlag I decided to return it in the evening. This I did; of course they were all rather concerned and soon threw me out again, but here I am in the saddle once more, have no pains despite the long day, only feelings of fatigue which is understandable, can work again and am immensely, immensely pleased that I have recovered by my own decision. I can't really explain it to myself, but it is a fact. Not that I expect the pains and the difficulties in walking to have completely disappeared by tomorrow, but if they are no worse than they were after my bold attempt today, I will be able to work and soon it will be gone for good.

Goodnight, my little princess, and not another word about my sciatica. I will add a few lines tomorrow.

Thursday, March 20, early

You vain little worm. You were ashamed of your photograph, and quite unreasonably! I don't have to mention how it is bound to please the one person who loves you; what I will mention is that it is more conducive than any other picture to inspiring respect in everyone else.

Any bad results of yesterday's venture ought to show themselves today. However, I am quite well, completely without pain, and have only some feelings of fatigue in the leg.

I think we can now put an end to this chapter in our correspondence. Today I am planning to go to the instrument-maker and start a new account. You can see how reckless I am, but I now have to take some risks. After that I have to do a little job that should bring me in fifteen gulden. Then I intend to refloat my four or five ships in the laboratory; apart from this I am going to stay at home and read. This is how I expect to spend the next ten days.

If Breuer doesn't turn up today, I am going to surprise him in the evening. Only yesterday he said I wasn't ill enough to be treated like a patient.

I trust the little princess is not indisposed because she announces herself as being tired? Please don't take advantage of my inability, caused by my own illness, to grumble about your state of health. On the other hand, if being ill gives a man the advantage of receiving more letters from his dear sweetheart, then I shall go to bed again.

How do you like that threat?

With fondest greetings

Your

Sigmund

37
To Martha Bernays

Vienna, Saturday
March 29, 1884

Beloved sweetheart

If it were not against discipline I would say that there is no need to tell me when you aren't feeling well (but please note that I don't say it)—I can always recognize it so clearly in your letters. When writing your last letter you weren't well either, for your foreboding is exactly like those nightmares that torture one only when one is suffering from indigestion. Then on waking one is relieved that it was only a dream, and this is how we should .also behave, quite apart from the probability that you would have found another man, whereas I wouldn't have found a professor's daughter.

Heavens above, little woman, how innocent and good-natured you are! Don't you realize that this very science could become our bitterest enemy, that the irresistible temptation to devote one's life without remuneration or recognition to the solving of problems unconnected with our personal situation, could postpone or even destroy our chances of sharing life—if I, yes, if I were to go and lose my head over it? Now, this is out of the question; I feel in fine fettle and intend to exploit science rather than allow myself to be exploited in its favor. I have been anxious during these weeks only because my experiments with brain anatomy comprise my only work. By the time you read this I shall be back on duty, busy with patients, and the new electrical appliances will help to keep me in the clinic.

The experiments are going well, by the way; I find myself in the position of making a few important assertions, partly confirming Meynert's disputed discoveries, partly new explanations which I feel sure will increase, and I hope all this will lead to some more good papers. My only embarrassment is what to do about Hollander: we had agreed in the beginning to publish the paper together, but now it would be far better for me to work on my own, for not only is his usefulness in this work far less than mine, he is no use whatever. He is quite incapable of adjusting himself to things, he turns up every two weeks for a couple of days, gets hold of a slide, lights a cigar (which one should never do in this work), reads a book (which one should also never do), then declares that the problems are very difficult—they are, thank God, otherwise anyone could do them—or that the light is too bad, then drops everything again and off he proudly strides. Good fellow though he is, his dilettantism inspires little respect. He behaves moreover, like a *grand seigneur,* takes no part in the technical work, whereas I work almost every evening till eleven or midnight, and it is not only that he is no use to me, I don't need him, either.

Since we are in the midst of scientific matters, one more word about the *Dozentur.* There is no salary attached to it, but two kinds of advantages. First the right (actually the only duty) to give lectures on which, if they are well attended whatever this depends on! I could manage to live, and this would enable me to relieve my poor harassed friend Breuer. Secondly, one rises to a higher social level in the medical world and in the eyes of the public, has more prospects not only of getting patients but of better-paying ones in short, it helps one to build up a certain reputation. Admittedly, there are also *Dozenten* without patients and in spite of the fair success of my labors our whole future does indeed still look rather dark. At least we will do everything in our power, and it will come out all right. . .

On Monday the thirty-first it will be three years since I became an M.D.; it hasn't brought me in anything so far, but it takes a lot to finish off a doctor, especially one with a precious sweetheart who protects him from idleness and silly escapades.

With the best wishes for my little princess's health

Your
Sigmund

38
To Martha Bernays

Vienna, Tuesday, at the Journal,
April 15, 1884

My sweet beloved

What a strange turn things are taking! As you say, "all must change, and live." I am returning your optimism with news that may signify this kind of change. I don't like grandiloquence, even though I am very deeply moved. In any case, let us say it seems we have started on the second volume of our highly interesting family chronicles (Riches). Just listen, it really sounds like a chapter out of Dickens: Paneth and his bride have invested in my name a capital sum of fifteen hundred gulden, of which the interest of eighty four gulden a year is to be used for an annual trip to Wandsbeck, which sum however is to be at my disposal at any time, especially if I were to take a decisive step towards our union by starting, say, a medical practice here or in the country, or by emigrating to America. Of this "foundation", the interest from which had already started as of April 1, only you are supposed to know. Even the Schwabs know nothing about it. Paneth broke the news to me today and we exchanged some very friendly words in the process. The idea behind it is to enable our marriage to take place six or even twelve months earlier.

These are so much to say about all this which I will let you guess, my darling. In any case I am heavily burdened with obligations towards other people, so much so that it rather oppresses me. But isn't it wonderful that normally parsimonious persons should be moved by the power of their and our true love to become warm and willing to make sacrifices? And isn't it wondered again that a wealthy man should mitigate the injustice of our poor origins and the unfairness of his own favored position? And think of how much happier and capable of work I shall be when we have you at my side! And then I will work and earn so much that I shall no longer need to feel ashamed.

With this gesture Paneth is entitled to make a greater claim on my friendship, needless to say there was no question of the loan being provoked, and my only regret us that I seriously believe I won't be able to enjoy this friendship very long. I shall have to thank her verbally or in writing. And as is even novel there are always two or several couples and intrigues, so something new happened this very day to Schonberg, too; something good and actually more honorable than that which happened to me. Buhler told him that Prof. Monier

126

Williams of Oxford wants to have Schonberg with him as soon as the middle of May, and so he has to take his degree in the haste, for which Buhler is offering him every possible facility. I do not think, though, that he will have to take a few weeks longer so as to not to overwork himself. I understand that his salary will be nothing up to £150 pounds, and that there is a possibility of his name being mentioned in the title of the dictionary on which he is collaborating. He will be seeing you all earlier than I. In any case Minna should be very please and will realize that this rare stroke of luck is not fair on an ordinary person.

And now your letter, the best, most beautiful you have ever written me, the most valuable, a letter that puts an end to all my doubts. Let us love one another and work.

With fondest greetings
From your
Sigmund

39

To Martha Bernays

Vienna, Saturday, at the Journal,
April 19, 1884

My precious Marty

Most certainly you can take seriously what I said, and please don't believe for a moment that I am making any sacrifices for you which you cannot think about with a free heart. Believe me, it is only natural that I should object more than you to the protracted waiting; I just stand it less well; it is a general rule that brides are happier than bridegrooms. So it is more for my own sake that I have decided on a short term career, and besides I am quite well convinced that your eyes-- the part must stand for the whole-- that you, my darling, will compensate me for a great deal; you too must believe this. And what am I sacrificing for it? I haven't gotten particularly far, and in the two years we still have to wait nothing very decisive is likely to happen. At best a slight change in my position in society. It won't cost me any effort; on the contrary, I will be only too happy to give up what is unimportant, of uncertain value and prospect in favor of something so worthy, refreshing and rich in sharing life with a beloved who is going to be not only a housekeeper and a cook but a precious friend and a cherished sweetheart as well. Add to this what I have often written to you, that in one field of science I am independent enough to make contributions without any further contacts or assistance, but which I mean my knowledge of the nervous stem, and I am happy to think that you will be able to help me with it. So the world will not be allowed to forget my name just yet. The trouble is I have so little ambition. I know I am someone, without having to b told so.

By a German region I was of course thinking of Lower Austria, Moravia or Silesia.

For the time being anyhow, I am still quite ready to fight and have no intention of breaking off my battle for the future in Vienna. The "struggle for existence" still means struggle for existence here. This past week the chances of being a *Dozent* next winter have, I must admit very remote. Owing to my medical activates with Frau S., I have hardly been able to do any work at all. No doubt I shall be able to buy clothes with fifty odd gulden, but I would far rather have spent this time going short of things with more chances to work. Bettelheim has brought the instruments; I myself bought another one today- i.e., paid the half; on Monday I expect the whole thing will start. But I am afraid the brain anatomy has been terribly neglected, nor has the preliminary work for my next publication gone very far. Frau S. is better again today; I hope during the next week to improve her health sufficiently treating her. The only unpleasant symptom is an old but suspicious catarrh of the lung which has affected one apex. If this gets worse, or if it proves to be connected with general illness, then the outlook is bad. I don't anticipate this, however, and believe that the restored heart will hold out for a while until another fainting fit gets her down again. But this might not happen for years.

I must ask you to forgive me for taking so long to talk about your situation. I am so sorry about it. Don't you at least take turns with Minna and go into the air a little? Marty, if you get ill over this I shall make a big fuss and you will see that it is not only patients but also lovers who can be very egoistic. The consultant's verdict doesn't impress me very much; I cannot see any reason why this business should last forever or return. Nor why the consultant should appear without being called, dropping in is not considered etiquette.

Shall I send you a book by Fritz Reuter? Reading aloud might perhaps help you over a few difficult hours?

Please write again soon, my darling, and tell me that you have been out-- provided your weather is less awful than ours is here.

With affectionate greetings
Your
Sigmund

40

To Martha Bernays

Vienna, Monday, at the Journal;
April 21, 1884

You will certainly be surprised, my darling, to hear that I am sitting here again after having written to you as recently as Saturday from the same spot; this result of my having been absent through being laid up so long, and rather awkward it is, too. I feel there is something altogether missing at the moment; I cannot work in the laboratory because of the prospering practice; work on the experiments, from which I expect little recognition, is lying idle.—it gave me quite a turn today when the proofs of my paper on method arrived from Leipzig; since then, with the exception of two small discoveries, I have done no work whatsoever. But otherwise I am very well, feel fitter than ever, I also love you even more that during our best days here, and if I write to you rarely, it is because of the beastly combination of being on duty and work at the Journal during these past few days; even yesterday, Sunday, I was in harness. Paneth was here today and told me that I may perhaps be summoned to a nervous case in Schwechat. Alois Schönberg has mentioned the prospect of a job in Pest. All these are simple beginnings, which do not necessarily have to materialize but they are nonetheless beginnings. Frau S. is much better now, I would be very pleased if nothing happened and I could stop treating her in a week's time. I would then advise her to go to the country at once.

I am toying now with a project and a hope which I will tell you about; perhaps nothing will come out of this, either. It is a therapeutic experiment. I have been reading about cocaine, the effective ingredient of coca leaves, which some Indian tribes chew in order to make themselves resistant to privation and fatigue. A German has tested this stuff on soldiers and reported that it has really rendered them strong and capable of endurance. I have now ordered some of it and for obvious reasons am going to try it out on cases of heart disease, then on nervous exhaustion, particularly in the awful condition following withdrawal of morphine) as in the case of Dr. Fleischl). There may be any number of other people experimenting on it already; perhaps it won't work. But I am certainly going to try it and as you know, if one tries something often enough and goes on wanting it, one day it may succeed. We need no more than one stroke of luck of this kind to consider setting up house. But, my little woman, do not be too convinced that it will come off this time. As you know, an exploder's temperament requires two basic qualities: optimism in attempt, criticism in work.

Now that I have talked out everything concerning myself, I shall come to you my precious girl. No I am still here. I don't even consider seeing you in the spring, I would like to have achieved something really good before we meet again. And this is what I am looking forward to more than I can say.

I am expecting the mailman today with the parcel and money; it looks as though he isn't coming, but this doesn't mean that you will have to wait long for your visiting cards and your seal. It is so nice of you to have expressed a wish; the fact that you are taking walks in the woods also pleases me very much. All alone, my Marty? Yesterday Dolfi said how very nice it would be if one day you could say, proudly of course: "I have waited four years for my husband." By the way, Marty, little Pauli has already fallen happily in love, what do you think of that? With the 28-year-old brother of her girlfriend, Glaser, with whom she used to spend her vacations. He has taken his law degree and is a junior counselor-at-law in our town Neutitschein in Moravia. Anyway a serious-sounding person. What do you think of it? Keep it to yourself, for I don't mean to say that the girl has definitely committed herself; but doesn't it look as though our silly girls are very much in demand? Dolfi is the only one still unattached. Yesterday—I had invited her to tea to get her to mend my black coat—she said: "It must be wonderful to be the fiancée of a cultured man, but a cultured man wouldn't want me, would he?" I couldn't help laughing at this category.

The mailman has just arrived, Marty; he brought very few nice things, but a letter containing 28 florins. It does a man good to have some money, darling; now another ten florins are coming to you; I shall hold onto them for a while, for I have no other money, but they are yours. Now what plans have you for your wardrobe? A jersey jacket? Are they still in fashion?

I am holding onto the money for a while not because I am stingy, but because the cocaine will cost something and because I impoverished myself yesterday by paying ten florins for an electric apparatus.

Now the apparatus are all there and we begin work tomorrow. I am seeing Frau S. only once a day. Schonberg is hard at work on Kant and Horace, but looks well and is in good form. Marty, doesn't all this together look rather like a second volume?

Now please write to me as much about yourself as I have of myself. And also whether you are well, completely well. Whether the iron is doing you good and whether you are drinking any wine. I shall be angry if you don't say yes to both.

You wanted to return something in my last letter. What was it?

Fondest greetings
Your
Sigmund

41

To Martha Bernays

**Vienna, Thursday,
May 29, 1884**

My darling, my precious darling, so this is how you neglect me? Two long days without a letter, and only because I failed you for a similar time? Don't you grant me this little privilege? If only you knew how things have been accumulating here, things of which I am the center, how the world has been bringing pressure on me from all sides! And you, darling, surely you should have time for me, even if once in a while I have none for you. But I don't want to be angry, you probably have a reason too, but it isn't mustn't be because you are not well, or because you don't love me.

Tuesday evening there was a Club meeting and Nothnagel invited me to accompany him. This was rather less than I had expected; I would have preferred to spend an evening in his room. What he said on the way also felt rather short of my expectation, or perhaps matched my earlier ones. I am afraid there won't be a golden snake, child, but it was a step forward all the time. You had better judge for yourself. It amounted to what we call "Etzes," and I would like to have told him so. He began reminding me that I am engaged and twenty-eight years old, and that I surely don't want my engagement to last another five or five years? "No." Nothn: "Well in that case I suggest the best thing for you to do would be to go to a provincial town, make a fortune there, and then—when, say, Breuer retires—come to Vienna. (May my friend Breuer, I thought to myself, go on working for many a year and not think of retiring.) You know how hard it is to get along in Vienna, how hard our colleagues work from morning to night and still barely eke out a living. Ah, there was a cousin of mine, for instance—he was my assistant in Jena and already a *Privatdozent*—he got engaged and so had to abandon his academic career and start a practice. 'Go to Nauheim,' I told him; 'a few years there and you will be a rich man.' No, he had to go to Berlin; there he is now, stuck, and can't get any further." Fr: "But, Herr Hofrat, an Austrian provincial town is not like a German town." Nothn: "All right, perhaps I don't know the conditions here; then it might be a good idea to go abroad. I could give you some recommendations to Buenos Aires, where a former assistant of mine has a practice; or to Madrid, where I have a number of connections. Fr: "Yes, I also consider emigrating, but first I want to try and see if I can't get along here. I have the capacity to work, and I am tied here by other things that the proximity of these beautiful buildings." Nothn: "How do you imagine going about it?" Fr: "I intend to apply for a *Dozentur* \; most of my papers are theoretical; would that be a disadvantage?" Noth: "No, as long as there are some clinical ones among them." Fr: "There would be, then I shall spend a certain time, say six months, seeing how the lecture courses develop and whether I can get the kind of practice that could be expected by someone with a minor reputation in the hospital; and if this doesn't work, then I'll get right out." Nothn: "Now, you must realize how difficult it is to get anywhere with these lectures. As you know, if a man is not in official position, people come flocking to him, whether he is a blockhead or not. But when a man without a position begins lecturing, he may well fare as I did when I started in Breslau. In my first course I had four students. You won't have any more, and will have to wait a long time before a course of this kind pays its way. If you want to remain in Vienna you'll have to count at best three years before being able to set up house. And if you had to leave after all, you would have to start all over again from scratch. How much do you think you'll need at first?" Fr: "I think I could manage with three thousand florins." Nothn: "I see you are well informed. Three to four thousand gulden, that's the minimum, and even then think how economically you would have to live!" Fr: "That doesn't apply to people who have been brought up the way I have, Herr Hofrat." Nothn: "I wasn't brought up any differently; I have known all kinds of privation; even as an assistant my lunch for the first six months consisted of two boiled eggs and for a long time afterwards all I had for supper was a piece of bread and a glass of water." (Then Nothnagel began again) : "Well, the electrotherapy idea isn't bad. There's room for someone in addition to Rosenthal and Benedikt, as Weiss's example has shown. Eulenberg, who might have been a competitor, isn't coming here either, and I don't imagine you are afraid of Weiss's brother. So I suggest you go on working as before, but the papers you have done up to now won't be of any use to you; general practitioners, on whom everything depends, are prosaic people who will think to themselves: 'What's the good of Freud's knowledge of brain anatomy? That won't help him treat a radialis paralysis!' You have to show them you can do that, too, have to give lectures to the Medical Association, publish clinical papers." Fr: "I intend to do all that and I'm in the midst of writing these papers." Nothn: "Well, that's good; you'll have to go on writing your papers for other reasons, but you can build up a practice only if general practitioners send you patients for electrical treatment."

By this time we had reached his house, where he said, "Goodbye, dear Freud"; I thanked him and went my way feeling rather depressed. All this good advice I have known myself for ages; he evidently thought he was dealing with a helpless person and even admitted his surprise at my being so well informed. The one valuable assurance, that he would send me patients, he failed to give me. But to judge from the whole situation, there is no doubt that he will do so, just as he talked of the *Dozentur* as something certain. At least he wasn't patronizing. I explained the contrast between his former warmth and today's reticence by the fact that as a stubborn and trusting man he clings to what his colleagues have told him as well as to what Breuer and Fleischl have said about me. Hence the certain impersonal interest he showed in speaking to me. The meeting, however, has been in advance, if not in Fleischl's sense, then in that of Breuer, whose interpretation has proved to be correct. I have no personal relationship with him.

Afterwards I went to Breuer, who had not been at the Club, so as to recover from my disappointment. They are both dear, good, and understanding friends. We talked till 1 A.M. She always insists on my taking a small apartment before long and hanging out a sign, just a sign, a beautiful sign.

I have so much more to tell you, but I had better send this letter off; you have been waiting long enough already. Your precious letter arrived early this morning; it did me a world of good; do write soon again....

It's all alright, I won't bring you anything, but I expect you to ask something from me when I am there.

Fond Whitsun greetings, darling. What memories this season brings back—precious, lovely ones, and some bitter ones as well. If only you had stayed here! Your leaving will have cost me a part of my life. I shall be with you for your birthday after all.

Once more a fond Whitsun greeting from

Your
Sigmund

42
To Martha Bernays

Vienna, Thursday,
June 19, 1884

My beloved treasure,

I can't remember having been so much rushed, otherwise I would have answered all your sweet, good letters with long pages of explanation; but as it is I have to be brief today, too; after all, I hope we will soon be able to talk.

Coca wasn't finished till last night; the first half has already been corrected today; it will be 1 ½ sheets long; the few gulden I have earned by it I had to subtract from my pupil, whom I sent away yesterday and today. Now there is still the correction of a second paper in addition I have to give electrical treatments, read, and work at the Journal, but I am as strong as a lion, gay and cheerful, and you can well imagine that this isn't the mood in which to drop everything and become a male nurse to a mental case.

My beloved girl, you must utterly banish drop your mind gloomy thoughts such as that you are hindering me from earning a living. After all, you know the key to my life: that I can work only when spurred on by great hopes for things uppermost in my mind. Before I met you I didn't know the joy of living, and now that "in principle" you are mine, to have you completely is the one condition I make to life, which I otherwise don't set any great store by. I am very stubborn and very reckless and need great challenges; I have done a number of things which any sensible person would be bound to consider very rash. For example, to take up science as a poverty stricken man, then as a poverty-stricken man to capture a poor girl—but this must continue to be my way of life; risking a lot, hoping a lot, working a lot. To average bourgeois common sense I have been lost long ago. And now I am supposed to not see you for three months—and this in addition to our uncertain circumstances, and with people as unpredictable as our families! In three months Eli maybe be in Hamburg, or the situation in my family may prevent me from leaving. In short, I know nothing about the future. I daren't count on it, but what I do know is that I need the refreshment of holding you in my arms again as urgently as I need food and drink; I know perfectly well that I have inflicted upon you enough worry and privation and mustn't rob you of our few happy weeks together, even if you were willing to renounce them yourself. I am going to follow my impulse and continue my venture; I want to strengthen myself through you and then with renewed strength go on trying to improve my position rather than tear myself away from all work for three months. The latter would have no great advantage; what I would save in money I would lose in time, and not much money would be saved anyway. Could you imagine me having a thousand gulden in the drawer and letting Rosa and Dolfi go hungry? Atleast half of it I would give it to them and the rest would be just sufficient to make up for the time I would have lost. It's true, they will be the losers, but I have to do the one thing that is right for my nature and our situation. I am completely of one mind about this.

Paneth came today, also convinced of course of the necessity of my accepting the job, but I possess the good quality of being able to believe in my own judgment. I have also found a number of people who agree with me. Anyhow, my darling, I know I shall be seeing you again before very long. Keep well; I must stop, for again there is a paper to correct.

Your
Sigmund

43
To Martha Bernays

Vienna, Sunday,
June 29, 1884

My beloved sweetheart

You are quite right. From now on I too will write only about the journey. I can no longer think of anything else. If you really insist on meeting me at the station, I cannot stop you. I was against it because I don't want to station and the luggage to get mixed up with our first kisses. But if you are not embarrassed by the serious Hamburgers and will give me a kiss as soon as I see you, ad on our way back to Wandsbek a second one, and a third, etc., then I will give in. I won't be tired because I shall be travelling under the influence of coca, in order to curb my terrible impatience.

Do rent a little room for me, very close to you and very modest, otherwise I will grumble that you are not being economical; if possible a little attic, I give you unlimited powers to decide.

My wardrobe won't be very grand, but respectable. I have a gray suit which I am now wearing, and a dark one which is still at the tailor's, a new overcoat and hat. For shirts I am rather badly off; I was going to buy some here, but Father suggested I buy them in Hamburg, where everything is better and cheaper, and what's more, you understand what one should buy.

I still haven't gotten my leave, will have to fight for it, if necessary will threat to quit altogether, but I have no doubt that I shall get it. I hear that Anna is now leaving Wandsbek already on the tenth, in which case I shall come a few days earlier, for my pupil will probably release me on the tenth, certainly not before; perhaps even later if I stay longer, and since each day brings in three florins this cannot be despised.

Cocaine runs to 25 pages, ready only today; you will see it before you see me. You know what I have been working on today.

Let us not worry about the weather. If it rains we can sit together and talk and read. I am going to bring a few good books on neurology; apart from this branch of science. I want to forget everything connected to Vienna in your presence. For you I will not bring anything, girl, but you will be having your birthday while I am there. I am very undecided whether to hand over the money and the bookkeeping to you or keep accounts myself. I think I shall save you the trouble and not let the control pass out of my hands too early. For two and occasionally three people the sum is not very impressive. On the contrary, if I can still scrape something together I shall do so. I have to leave something for my family. Dolfi seems to need a little for herself. Yesterday I took her to the Prater; for the first time I was the rich man of the family. Rosa leaves today for Oberwaltersdorf with Herzig for three weeks. Dolfi and Pauli have jobs starting on the fifteenth. Father is bearing up, but he has a lot of troubles. Oh, girl, I must become a rich man and then when they want something they will have to come to you.

Your
Sigmund

44
To Martha Bernays

Vienna, Monday,
June 30, 1884

My beloved girl,

I am so glad we now see eye to eye and that you won't have to reproach yourself for anything while waiting for me. I am also so happy in anticipation of the beautiful days we are going to spend together. I know that at this point you want to interrupt: I must not anticipate anything so as to avoid disappointment. But, Marty, the beauty of these days depends on ourselves alone and not on the weather, not on the moods of other people, nor on the good or bad news that may come in the meantime. I want to bring back from the journey nothing but the certainty, the final conviction that you are utterly mine—in your attitude, great love, and all the little signs of affection. To take a retrospective glance as you do is quite justified; I really think I have always loved you much more than you me, or, more correctly: until we were separated you hadn't surmounted the *primum falsum* of our love—as a logician would call it—i.e., that I forced myself upon you and you accepted me without any great affection. I know it has finally changed and this success, which I wanted more than anything else, and the prolonged absence of which has been my greatest misery, gives me hope for the other successes which I still need.

Do you remember how you often used to tell me that I had a talent for repeatedly provoking your resistance? How we were always fighting, and you would never give in to me? We were two people who diverged in every detail of life and who were yet determined to love each other, and did love each other. And then, after no hard words had been exchanged between us for a long time, I had to admit to myself that you were indeed my beloved, but so seldom took my side that no one would have realized from your behavior that you were preparing to share my life; and you admitted that I had no influence over you. I found you so fully matured and every corner in you occupied, and you were hard and reserved and I had no power over you. This resistance of yours only made you the more precious to me, but at the same time I was very unhappy, and when at the corner of the Alser Strasse we said goodbye for thirteen months, my hopes were very low, and I walked away like a soldier who knows he is defending a lost position. And whereas our being together threatened to estrange us, during the separation I received signs that I might be victorious after all—not from any abundance of tender words, not from the fulfillment of any wish—I myself don't know how, but I did notice that I was beginning to mean something else to you, that the stiffness and reserve which you yourself so often deplored would vanish the moment we were together. And since then I too have become another person, many wounds that went deeper than you knew have been closed, and I feel within me a gaiety and a self-confidence which for a whole year had been unknown to me. And for this reason I don't want to postpone strengthening myself for new tasks by the long-desired happiness of a close harmony with you. Only occasional whispered doubts crop up: if at the moment you love so fondly the me whom you haven't seen for such a long time and then you see me again, see the gesture, hear the voice and the opinions which invariably used to arouse your defiance, won't you discover that your fondness was directed at an idea that you made for yourself, and not at the living person who perhaps will have upon you the same effect he did a year or two ago? The "no" to this, my love, I can only experience and I am waiting so impatiently for it. Waiting is as much as my fate as yours. To wait in peace and in resignation, or to wait in the midst of struggle and agitation—the difference is not so great, no greater than our different way of facing the world. Another two weeks—but further I refuse to think. The years beyond are hidden from me as though by a screen. I love you so much and am longing to hear from you that you love me too, and I want to spend four weeks that are not sacrificed to the future, as all time hitherto has been, but which are the future itself.

I trust that you are well again, my sweet child? I have never felt better, and I now miss the work. I must think how best to spend the next two weeks. Probably writing reviews for periodicals and regular daily observation of patients. I am very much respected in the department.

Tuesday, July 1, 1884

My sweet treasure

The new month has begun with rain, but in my case with high spirits and good news. And I am hoping to experience so many lovely things before it ends.

My darling, I have been interrupted so many countless times, I must stop, which I do with fondest greetings and happiest expectations. It is even possible that something nice can be acquired for your birthday; a pupil in brain anatomy has been suggested to me; he wants to take a four week course; I am going to offer him one of only two weeks. If he comes and accepts it, it will mean quite a bit of money, and then we will go for a walk through Hamburg and look for something Marty wants. What's more, I may get a free ticket through Franceschini as far as the border, in which case I shall be able to leave a little something for my family. Coca appeared today, but I haven't seen it yet.

I hope there is nothing in this letter that offends you, my sweet Marty? If so, you must tell.

Your
Sigmund

45
To Martha Bernays

Vienna, Sunday,
August 3, 1884

My sweet Princess

Things are so unevenly distributed, I have my work if not to comfort me at least to stupefy me, and you have nothing but my picture. I wonder what it tells you? How I wish I could let you know what I'm thinking and hoping! Long, indescribable intense happiness if only you keep well. I am always hearing that you look pale. My pale little princess—and four weeks; but stop, I am not to talk about it.

I am writing today to send you two small bits of good news, or at least that is what I consider them. First, that I will get the specimen of my beautiful diagnosis which has cause considerable sensation here, so I shall be able to write quite a nice paper on it; second, that Dr. Heitler has returned and that we have decided to take our money to the instrument-maker tomorrow to buy what we need and then work very hard so as to finish the electrical experiment. Aren't you please, my darling? Work, nothing but work; I myself am surprised at the amount of work I can get through. But I know what's driving me; the heart is well again, the giant strong again, gigantically strong. Are you laughing at me for calling myself a giant? Sometimes I have such sense of power I feel there must be something I could still do to bring us together sooner. How I will love you then, laugh at you and scold you, and you won't say a word, because you are a silent darling.

I received the second warm letter from Hammerschlag; he inquires among other things whether you have firmly decided to take a job here and says that apart from his interest for me he has an additional one—just what I cannot guess. He also says that if Tedesco's daughters have inherited a single characteristic from their mother, whom he knows, then a job with one of them would be very pleasant.

I will write to Fleischl sooner, tomorrow morning, and add that you won't be free till the end of September. If the lady hasn't found anyone yet, she will probably wait till she returns from the country. If this doesn't work, then we will find something else. Breuer, Fleischl, Schwab, Hammerschlag—my friendly guard will help.

August 4, Evening

I broke off yesterday to finish the department's statistical report for July and today I can respond to your sweet letter which reminds me of our most peaceful days. Oh, I could echo the words of Heine's shepherd boy: "It is a weary task to reign…" etc., except that my queen is still only a princess.

You will know by now that whatever happens I am all in favor of your leaving; once you are free we will live so happily, each of us serving and working, each in a state of constraint and renunciation, but happy nevertheless. I just cannot imagine what it will feel like not to be separated from each other by two days.

I received the specimen today and will soon have a drawing made of it. The publication will take three to four months because the microscopic examination has to be finished first. I am thinking that when I return from my trip I will be able to work better still and that when you come to see me we will shut the door, you will sit close beside me and lean against my shoulder while I go on working till I am tired and longing to kiss you. Just now a patient to whom I have been giving very successful electrical treatment for buzzing in the ear promised me of the most beautiful fruit for "my young woman", the lady whom I certainly must have—she refrained from saying "sweetheart" out of respect. Actually, she is the fruit seller from The Three Ravens, where one turns off to the Seitenstättengasse.

We don't have to worry about the cholera, my darling; it is not likely to prevent my leaving here in September; instead, I think it will arrive here suddenly next year.

Rumor has it that Breuer has again applied for a vacant position in Primarius in the hospital I would be delighted if he succeeded, then I would do everything to become *Sekundararzt* and learn a lot. But he won't get it.

How are you feeling sweet darling? At least you are better off than I am. When you read this it will already be the sixth of August; I am writing this only on the fourth of this endless month.

With fondest greetings and kisses
You Sigmund

Please thank Minna very much

46
To Martha Bernays

Vienna, Thursday,
August 14, 1884

My sweet little princess

I am taking the liberty of pointing out that there are only seventeen more days and that between the time I write this and you read it half of this wretched month will have been slain. May we never have another like it! Amen.

I am pleased to detect from the tone of our letter a note of returning calm and well-being. Let us be wonderfully well when we meet in seventeen days. I am afraid this second journey won't be quite like the first; all kinds of little things are missing. First, the belief—I won't believe it till I am actually sitting in the train. Then I am rather more tired, my best suit is so worn I hardly dare travel in it, and I will have only the second one in which to parade in Wandsbek. It is really mostly stains that spoil it, and perhaps been something can be done about this. My hat is no longer new, I have been obliged to buy shirts here, of an inferior quality, but my love us the same and the longing has increased. I am not working so hard nowadays, am almost lazy, although I am busy all day, but I am sure of the new contacts when I return, and all my old papers have at last appeared. The most recent one I sent you was an amplification of a previous work, the best I have ever done, although so far I haven't received one word of recognition for it, nothing but reproaches for the alleged lack of references to the relevant literature. At the moment I have nothing in print but all kinds of things in my head.

Rosa was here yesterday, was seen by several colleagues and made a great impression with her beauty. Poor thing, she is leaving in a few days for Frau Königstein in Gmunden. Tomorrow I am going home for once to take the family out. Today the Hammerschlags, the dear people, are celebrating their silver wedding. Yesterday I sent them a photograph of myself. AS soon as I get some more, I will send one to Minna; who can resist flattery? It will interest her to hear that Frau P., with whom she was in Italy, has died.

Tomorrow there is going to be a simple church service to celebrate the centenary of this hideous, grandiose building which was founded by Emperor Joseph. I am not likely to go; it doesn't fit in with my time and I am not anxious to hear a Mass. Till the first of September I am wound up and then I will unwind, then I hope the visit to my sweet princess will supply me with a new spring.

With fondest greetings

Your
Sigmund

47
To Martha Bernays

Vienna, Sunday,
August 17, 1884

My girl

That was sweet of you; what a lovely scent these flowers have, what memories they evoke! They life me out of all the litter of my bookish, bachelor life! And at the same time wan me that summer is coming to an end that we will have to hurry if we are to enjoy the autumn. And this I will certainly take to hearth and nothing is going to stop me. Roughly another two weeks! A week from today the chief is coming back, and the price I shall have to pay to return to you and come to my senses depends on his moo. No price will seem too high. I have changed more than I myself realized. Today four young hospital colleagues insisted on my joining them on an excursion to Dornbach. On our way back we stopped at the same inn where you and I once spent a quiet evening. I felt very out of place, I think I can feel happy nowadays only in your presence, and I cannot imagine that I shall ever be able to enjoy myself again without you. With the exception of the minutes brightened by your letters, I have experienced during the past fourteen months only three or four happy days—when some minor piece of work of mine happened to succeed. And that is too little for a human being who is still young and yet has never felt young. And because I know it is only your going away that has hurt me so much, I feel incapable of reconciling myself to her whose heartlessness and caprice I hold responsible for your departure. And this is something you will have understood long ago my darling.

But only another two weeks after all; I will manage to doze through the days, and then I will quench my thirst with your kisses and lead a very different life that will make both of us whole and young again, and when we have to separate once more we will do so with the confidence of never again taking upon us hardships such as we have endured these past fourteen months.

I have just had a letter from Mother, saying she is arriving at 4:30. Today, however, I am on duty.

With fondest greetings & kisses
Your
Sigmund

48
To Martha Bernays

**Vienna, at night,
September 30, 1884**

My sweet little woman

So you managed to get here first! Thank you so much for your dear letter which has just taken me by surprise. The post office must know I am back again. Everything here seems so strange; to think I am really no longer with you! It was so and it will be lovely again and remain so—no, even lovelier.

I have a whole bad full of news for you, big news and little news, but it would be useless to try and tell you it all now. Its 11:30 and I am very tired, but not mentally, in fact I am very fresh and very happy. No despondency whatever, I feel nothing but infinite gratitude to you, you dear, auspicious one! To my surprise I feel quite gay, more courageous, I would almost say more magnanimous; than before. I know I will work hard, put up with all sorts of difficulties, and that for a long time I will consider myself richly rewarded by the memory of our time together.

Just these few lines; don't consider this letter as completed; I just want to send you a sign of life. I had the most pleasant journey, have established myself again in the hospital, have been to Hammerschlag's and home, and now I am off to bed and send you my warm and fond greetings.

**Your
Sigmund**

Do I need to tell you that tomorrow I shall spend every free quarter of an hour writing to you?

Many thousand greetings. I am writing on a scrap of paper and an old envelope. I have just come across the confusion in my belongings.

49

To Martha Bernays

Vienna, Monday,
November 17, 1884

My sweet little woman

My fondest greetings for the seventeenth. We will soon have belonged to each other for 2 ½ years; to think that we have been waiting for each other all that time! I would be sad if I didn't know the fact that you are mine is far more important than the other fact—that you are not here at my side. You are so sweet and you are so far away, but I intend to dwell on the former.

> Dr. Leslie
> Dr. Darling
> Dr. Montgomery
> Dr. Giles
> Dr. Green.
> Dr. Campbell

Do you know what this means my precious? Have you read Don Quixote and do you remember the condition the hero makes to all the knights he has conquered? They have to walk to Toboso and kiss the hand of the incomparable Dulcinea. Now my six students are kissing you hand. Yes, my lecture course has become reality. Today I read—i.e., I lectured in English for a whole hour and demonstrated on a patient, and the little box which I brought on the Speersort contains a hundred self-earned gulden, of which I am sending you a sample. How good this tastes, girl! One of them, as a matter of fact, didn't pay; he is the organizer of the lectures, Dr. Leslie, whom of course I am only too pleased to take free of charge. But this evening he came to see me again and sang my praises, which I find suspicious. Do you think he is going to charge a commission at the end? I don't think so.

What am I going to do with all the money? From now on Marty and Minna are going to drink port; there will be a regular monthly contribution to my family; a pair of winter trousers can be ordered;

How wonderful! An isolated income of this kind doesn't make much difference to my budget, you know, but should the lectures continue regularly, girl, it will mean the end of the sponger's existence and the beginning of the end of the "Dalles."

I am so busy at the moment. Just think: the department, the lecture course and the difficult preparation for it, the work on the brain anatomy and the Ecgonin, for which nothing has been done during the past week—how is all this going to work out? I am going to economize both in time and money, and work vigorously and valiantly now that I see more chances of getting ahead.

Lustgarten is back and, what's more, as a great man with a great invention, but he is very friendly. He was only one day in Hamburg and very depressed at that time because he thought his discovery had miscarried; which is why he didn't come to see you. Oh, they have all outstripped me in game, but not in happiness and not in contentment so long as you are going to be mine.

Your
Sigmund

50

To Martha Bernays

Vienna, Thursday,
January 6, 1885

My precious darling

In the confusion of the past few days I haven't found a moment's peace to write to you. The hospital is in an uproar. You will hear at once what it is all about.

On Sunday Koller was on duty at the Journal, the man who made cocaine so famous and with whom I have recently become more intimate. He had a difference of opinion about some minor technical matter with the man who acts as the surgeon for Billroth's clinic, and the latter suddenly called Koller a "Jewish swine." Now the general bitterness—in short, we would all have reacted just as Koller did: by hitting the man in the face. The man rushed off, denounced Koller to the director who, however, called him down thoroughly and categorically took Koller's side. This was a great relief to us all. But since they are both reserve officers, he is obliged to challenge Koller to a duel and this very moment they are fighting with sabers under rather severe conditions. Lustgarten and Bettelheim (the regimental surgeon) are Koller's seconds.

I am too upset to write anymore now, but I won't send this letter off till I can tell you the result of the duel. SO much could be said about all this.—

Your pleasure over the little presents made me very happy; surely Minna wouldn't think that I would confine her to a calendar! The Eliot is for her, I have reminded them again. As for money, my little woman, you keep it; Minna has a claim to part of the previous sum; it will be a long time before either of you get more.

Paneth has given me six bottles of very good wine, some of which will go to my family, but some will be drunk by myself and others here in my room. One bottle has gone off today to Koller to fortify him for the fight. I am considering a reckless purchase. For the forty-two florins' interest from Paneth I am going to buy myself a decent silver watch with a chronograph in the back; it has the value of a scientific instrument, and my old wreck of a think never keeps proper time. Without a watch I am really not a civilized person. These watches cost forty florins.—I am too impatient to go on writing.

So far my neuralgia injections are working very well; the trouble is I have very few cases. Yesterday I went to see Prof. Weinlechner and Standhartner, who gave me permission to use the treatment on all cases of this king in their department. I hope to learn more soon about the value of the procedure.

I must go and see if they are back.

All is well, my little woman. Our friend is quite unharmed and his opponent got two deep gashes. We are all delighted, a proud day for us. We are going to give Koller a present as a lasting reminder of his victory.

Farewell, my sweetheart, and write again soon to

Your
Sigmund

51
To Martha Bernays

Vienna, Wednesday,
January 7, 1885

My beloved darling

At last a letter from you again, which makes me laugh, for it informs me that you now possess three copies of the article you wanted. No you can send one to Rosa.

On one point I cannot agree with you, Marty. You say how sensible we are now and how foolishly we treated one another in the past. I gladly agree that we are now sensible enough to believe in our love without any doubts, but we would never have reached this point had it not been for all that went before. It was the very intensity of my misery brought about by the many hours of suffering you caused you caused me two years ago and since, that convinced me of my love for you. Today, what with all the work, chasing after money, position, and reputation, all of which hardly allows me time to drop you an affectionate line, I could never reach that conviction. Let us not despise the times when for me a day was made worth living merely by a letter from you, when a decision from you meant a decision between life and death. I really don't know what else I could have done at that time; it was a difficult period of struggle and finally of victory, and only after it was all over could I find the inner peace to work towards our future. In those days I was fighting for your love as I am now for your person, and you must admit that I had to work as hard for the one as I am now for the other.—

During the past few days I have been feeling a bit of seedy, engaged as I am in the two fold struggle which forms the content of *Auch Einer*: struggle against a cold and against "the object." I have a combination of nose-throat-gums-ear catarrh and am correspondingly miserable. I suggest you read about it in Vischer.

My object has a specific name, it is called neuralgia—face-ache. The question is whether I shall succeed in curing it. I have already told you about one case which has very much improved; but now I am treating a second, a clear, much nicer case, at Prof. Weinlechner's. The result of the first day was very good. But what will the following days produce? I am so excited about it, for if it works I would be assure for some time to come of attracting the attention so essential for getting on in the world. Everything we hope for would be there and perhaps even Fleischl could benefit from it. And even if it isn't absolutely sensational, something is bound to come out of it.

I now have eleven subscribers for the lecture course, but wretchedly few cases, and I am continuously worried as to how I am to find the necessary material, but I will manage.

Yesterday evening I went to see Breuer, where I met Fleischl, who was very talkative but not in a particularly pleasant way. If only I could relieve him of the pain!

Goodnight, my little woman. You are quite right, it is sad that we cannot exchange kisses, only letters.

Your
Sigmund

52

To Martha Bernays

Vienna, Friday,
January 16, 1885

My sweet darling

A very affectionate greeting for the seventeenth; do you realize, by the way, that my lecture course also started on the seventeenth? And here, quickly, is my news, to make you happy at once. The die is cast. Today I had my wild beard trimmed and went to see Nothnagel, handed in my card: "take the liberty of asking if and when the Herr Hofrat can be seen on an important personal matter.: The usual crowd, usual anxious whispering among the people around me, whether I was a doctor and would be admitted before them who had already be waiting for too long. The conversation I understood best was between a lady in mourning and her brother. Her feminine eye immediately diagnosed something suspicious to me, whereas the brother with a superior smile contradicted her suggestion that I could be a member of that pernicious profession. At last came the disappointment, for I was admitted ahead of them all to the man who had so often played a decisive part in my life, and behind him once more the picture of the thoughtful, serious, dead woman. I asked whether he would like me to state my request now or later. If brief, now, he said. Otherwise it would be better to talk it over another time. I promised to be brief. "You once said you would be willing to assist me, and I believed it because it was you who said so. Now the opportunity has arrived. I would like to ask your opinion whether on the strength of my existing publications I should apply for the Dozentur or whether I should wait till I have more." "What are your papers on, Doctor? Coca—"(So coca is associated with my name.) I interrupted him to produce my collective writings, those from the pre Marty days and those of a later date. He just glanced at the number. "You seem to have eight or nine," he said. "Oh, by all means send in your application. When I think of the kind of people who get the Dozentur…! There won't be the slightest objection." "But I have several more things to be published, two of them in the immediate future." "You won't need them; these are more than enough." "But there isn't much about neuropathology among them." "That doesn't matter. Who knows anything about neuropathology unless he has studied anatomy and physiology? You do want the Dozentur for neuropathology, don't you? In that case three people will be chosen to report—Meynert, Bamberger, and probably myself. There won't be any opposition, and if any objection is raised on the faculty, sure we are men enough to put it through?" "So I may assume that you will support my application for the Dozentur? I know Meynert will." "Certainly, and I don't think there will be any objections; if there are, we'll push it through just the same." I added: "It's a question of legalizing an unauthorized lecture course I'm giving. Actually I'm only lecturing to some English people in their language, but there's quite a run on it." Then we shook hands warmly and off I went as the newest Dozent. I will send in my application next week. This time you won't miss your golden snake.

Let one fond kiss stand for many from...

Your
Sigmund

53

To Martha Bernays

Vienna, Wednesday,
January 21, 1885

My little sweetheart

All kinds of things have been happening, so forgive me if this is a bit muddled. There has been a rumor that the German Kaiser has died. But now he is supposed to be alive and will certainly outlive us all.

Today I handled in my application for the Dozentur and talked to Prof. Ludwig and Meynert. The latter was decidedly optimistic and also mentioned very suggestively the neurological ward on which he is counting. I have an idea that if he gets it he will take me. There must have been a lot of talk about me this evening. Fleischl has been invited to Meynert's and is going to put in a good word for me, while Ludwig has gone to a restaurant to work on the dangerous Kundradt, the pathological anatomist.

And now for you letter. There is a lot to answer in it. First, if I will allow myself to skate. Definitely not, I am too jealous for that. I myself cannot do it, and anyway wouldn't have the time to accompany you, and accompanied you would have to be. So drop that idea. Then I insist you on your buying a decent rug up to the price of twenty eight marks, which I will send you out of the earnings from my next lecture—at the moment I am quite poor. If you still have any money left, please use it for this purpose and I will pay you back.

Third, I really cannot see why you should be cold. Is there no stove, no wood in Wandsbeck? Explanation urgently required. I trust it won't again come to the point of your not being able to write to me in one room because it's too cold and in the other because you are too often disturbed. That was the most terrible letter I have ever had from you, and I certainly will not forget even if I live to be eighty-five and you were to give me a kiss every day, which is perhaps asking rather much! Darling, is it possible that you can be affectionate only in summer and that in winter you freeze up? Now sit down and answer me at once so that I will still have time to get myself a winter girl.

And what else? That you will have to pretty unlucky to miss the golden snake this time. Perhaps you don't know that the brides of Dozents are obliged to wear golden snakes to distinguish themselves from ordinary doctor's brides.

One other thing I want to say: Just because someone happens to cross our path, you mustn't call him a nasty character. Pfungen especially is quite within his rights, and there is nothing nasty about his intentions.—anyway, at the moment the worst has been avoided.

I intend to have a number of books bound. Beginning tomorrow, I am going to eat supper in my rooms. Otherwise I will get out of the habit of working in the evening.

Goodnight, little woman, be very good and love me a little bit.

Your
Sigmund

54
To Martha Bernays

Vienna,
March 10, 1885

My sweet darling

Woe to the day you became so rich that I, like a character in a bad novel, have to ask you politely whether you wish to continue to be my betrothed as I don't want to stand in theway of you happiness, etc. I am already looking forward to writing the letter and getting your answer—but I seem to remember that we already indulged in this kind of fantasy about a year ago. Don't you know, by the way, that only the poor have difficulty in accepting presents, never the rich?

Otherwise, my darling, I feel splendidly well, I am like "lucky Hans," today the last of my various affairs will be settled and then I shave a frightening amount of time, all the afternoon except one hour to use the ophthalmoscope, and the light is so good. I feel no desire to be lazy, I am in quite an industrious mood.—Today the application has been handed in, the case seems hopeless, although Lustgarten has put in a word for me with Prof. Ludwig, and perhaps it will lead to the new *Primarius'* forming a good opinion of me and allowing me to lecture in his department.

I brought the lectures to an end today; a lady arrived to sign up for the next, and I had to tell her there wasn't going to be one.

Today, you know, marks a clear dividing line in my life; all the old things have been finished, and I am in a completely new situation. But it has been a good time; I have only pleasant memories of the lectures; it wasn't just the money, but the learning and the teaching; and it has enhanced my reputation in the reputation in the hospital.

Shall I go and see Breuer today and say goodbye for the time I am going to dig myself in? I think I will. It is a long time since. I have felt so well as during these bad days and I have hardly ever looked so fit. I am not seeing the family now, it is too painful for me to admit my lack of money. They are aware of it, anyhow.

I am keeping on my old apartment this month, but I have changed my charwoman and feel all the better for it. I am now eating support in my own room, modestly, but I enjoy it, and I can make plans, read, and write reports to my heart's content.

I wrote to Fleischl yesterday. But did not insist on an answer because writing is so difficult for him. On Friday or Saturday, when I have come to an end of my money, I will go and see him. I wonder if he will lend me anything…

You don't write a word about Minna? I hope she will be all right when we meet again.

Fond greetings

Your
Sigmund

I give you the solemn promise that I will marry you even if you don't get the 1500 marks. If necessary, I will marry you with 150,000,000 marks.

55
To Martha Bernays

Vienna, Tuesday,
March 31, 1885

My sweet darling

Apart from your two charming letters, quite a number of pleasant things have come my way during the past few days on which I will now report to you in detail. First, my second paper on coca has been printed verbatim in a Zeniralblatt; second, I have received from Dr. Pritchard, whom you all know, a nice letter which I shall not fail to answer and which I herewith enclose. I am now especially pleased that I told him to go to Wandsbek. But then the most important thing: a few excellent discoveries in brain anatomy, five to six in number, which are to adorn my next big paper. Some of these things I am discovering are actually being published piecemeal every week by someone else (from Leipzig); but I am going to wait patiently till I have all the material together before starting my paper. I am not sure if I should count the following event among the pleasant ones. My successful rivals election for the position of Sekundararzt has not been confirmed by the local government because he is Hungarian, and from now on Hungarian are to be treated as foreigners. It is generally considered possible that the local government will appoint me in his place. But at the moment I have little desire to become once more part of the hospital establishment. What I was, as you know, is to go to Paris via Wandsbek, have enough leisure to finish my work on the brain, and then the independence to find out what chances there are for us here. If I do not accept the position I shall first of all not be able to finish the work on the brain; secondly, I will not be granted leave for the journey and so would have to abandon the position again in two months; this would simply have the effect of annoying Primarius Hein; on the other hand, if I renounce the journey and continue with the hospital routine, I would soon lose my patience. It's true of course, I haven't got the traveling grant yet; lots of people would say it is sheer folly to turn down a job I applied for a month ago. But a human being's demon is the best part of him, it is himself. One shouldn't embark on anything unless one feels wholehearted about it. What do you think? Let me know.

It is four years today since I got my doctor's degree, and I celebrated the occasion by doing nothing and paying a call on Breuer at noon. Work starts again tomorrow. I am very well and my Marty, too, I trust. If only I could see what she looks like. Would I recognize her in the street? Now and again I see a girl in the street who looks like her in one way or another, whereupon I invariably follow her for a while to convince myself she isn't here. She probably won't see Vienna again until she is my wife. If only this could be soon.

Is the wish of
Your
Sigmund

56
To Martha Bernays

Vienna,
April 28, 1885

My precious darling

To be angry with you for demanding a news in such an impatient fashion is difficult, and I am sure you are not serious about it. I am too happy in the knowledge that someone loves me, and that this someone is you. By now I hope you are reassured. You can always believe what I say; don't you know that yet? Oh, what a wicked girl you are! If I were feeling better I would try and take you to task, but I am so dreadfully tired that I would be very grateful for a few affectionate words from you. But they would take two days to reach me by then I hope to be over my tiredness.

Now I want to tell you about my minor projects. By the end of this week I will be relieved of my duty to consider myself a public danger. I expect the tailor to bring my summer suit on Saturday morning. If the weather is fine I shall at once board a train and ramble about on the Semmering for at least three days. Alone, without you, it cannot be beautiful; in fact, it is not meant to be a pleasure, simply a medicine. Before this, on the thirtieth, the chemist is to pay me for the research on cocaine. Now we must wait and see if everything works out according to plan.

This has been a bad, barren month. How glad I am it is soon coming to an end! I do nothing all day; sometimes I browse in Russian history, and now and again I torture the two rabbits which nibble away at turnips in the little room and make a mess of the floor. One intention as a matter of fact I have almost finished carrying out, an intention which a number of as yet unborn and unfortunate people will one day resent. Since you won't guess what kind of people I am referring to, I will tell you at once: they are my biographers. I have destroyed all my notes of the past fourteen years, as well as letters, scientific excerpts, and the manuscripts of my papers. As for letters, only those from the family have been spared. Yours, my darling, were never in danger. In doing so all old friendships and relationships presented themselves once again and they silently received the coup de grace (my imagination is still living in Russian history); all my thoughts and feelings about the world in general and about myself in particular have been found unworthy of further existence. They will now have to be thought all over again, and I certainly had accumulated some scribbling. But that stuff settles round me like sand drifts round the Sphinx; soon nothing but my nostrils would have been visible above the paper; I couldn't have matured or died without worrying about who would get hold of those old papers. Everything, moreover, that lies beyond the great turning point in my life, beyond our love and my choice of profession, died long ago and must not be deprived of a worthy funeral. AS for the biographers, let them worry, we have no desire to make it too easy for them. Each of them will be right in his opinion of "The Development of the Hero," and I am already looking forward to seeing them go astray.

This morning I went to see Fleischl; I had already been there twice, but he was asleep. His condition has not changed; he begins to give his lectures today, and I am wondering how he will stand it. He keeps a parrot in his room, a bird which means more to him than many a human being. It is a creature with plumage of outrageous colors to which he attributes all manner of subtleties, whereas I maintain that it is very stupid. The beast emits a kind of croaking sound which he interprets as *Bröckerl;* today to my surprise it actually uttered its name, Lore, several times. The animal does know one trick: it spreads its wings on order, allowing one to admire their beauty, but today Fleischl spent a good half hour imploring the bird to display them with the kind of ardor that normally a man might muster once in a lifetime for a girl; and the brute paid not the slightest attention. He couldn't help admitting that this behavior testified to bad character.

I have heard that Leidesdorf and Pollitzer have been won over to my side. I am expected to call on the latter, but not yet; I must first feel human again.

I greet you fondly and thank you for many letters.

Your
Sigmund

57
To Martha Bernays

Vienna, Wednesday,
April 29, 1885

Highly esteemed Princess

If you keep your word; there should be a letter from you tomorrow instead of a card, my sweet darling! I promise you that once we have got through this terrible period of waiting, you won't have to touch a pen for ten years. What do you think, shall we get married in August after I have got my *Dozentur*? I will have to take an apartment anyway and we are surely both eligible. Which reminds me: you never respond to such suggestions, you just let me talk and occasionally laugh at me—wont you for once kindly let me know what you think it is all going to be like, how long, how much, under what condition, and so on? So I expect a very detailed expose about our future.

I might add that today I feel once again in a healthy frame of mind, something like the high spirits of convalescence. So don't be annoyed, my darling. To be healthy is so wonderful if one isn't condemned to be alone. Well, once summer comes the sluggish waters will begin to stir.

Greetings and kisses from

**Your
Sigmund**

58
To Martha Bernays

Vienna, Thursday,
May 7, 1885

My precious Princess

Today my treasures arrived and gave me the greatest pleasure. I had expected the writing set to be much more complicated; it will certainly come in handy; the little prescription block is quite charming; I can hardly believe you managed it with so little advice, but I won't begin using it yet, it is too beautiful, not till I start my own practice. And finally, the crackers, they have a most wonderful spicy flavor; quite incredible that crackers can taste like that. While enjoying the tender care which you have lavished on me, a number of thoughts have occurred to me who can be summed up like this: preparation for marriage is like the writing of a paper: one never finishes it; one just has to set oneself a deadline and break off somewhere. And I for my part have decided that an end of our misery must be made on June 17, '87, that by then we must be man and wife, whether things are going well or badly or not at all. Why shouldn't we be able to endure some hardships together, and anyway for the first year we would be safe with your money—mine by the time would have been sent. The carrying out of this plan, which is meant very seriously, depends entirely on the consent of one person only—you, Marty.

Today I went to see the family and apart from this took a very bold step—went to Tischer and ordered the two suits I need so urgently. Do you approve? When they head who I am, I was received with open arms.

Goodnight, my sweet darling. It's 1:30 A.M.; the day has simply fled by. Hope to work tomorrow. The flowers are for Minna, and I hope there will be a letter for me tomorrow.

Your
Sigmund

59

To Martha Bernays

Vienna, Tuesday,
May 12, 1885

My precious little woman

I am delighted about the new yes in your last letter as I was about the first one. Let us arrange things as you suggest if it is at all possible. I realize of course that the time of worry and trouble won't come to an end even then, but I think you realize this too and will appreciate the fact that we shall be going though it together and that our greatest desire will have been fulfilled. This long waiting certainly makes us neither happier nor younger and, as you admit, it doesn't bring to us the end of worrying about our future. I take it that your consent is seriously meant and not inspired by some whim of the moment, and I am deeply happy about it; I can't express it in other words.

Now let me tell you what today I lectured for an hour in the Club on brain anatomy—actually for one person only, Prof. Obersteiner, because the others must have been very bored; but I enjoyed it and dealt not too badly with the difficult subject. I have also just written a letter to Prof. Mendel in Berlin, editor of neurological journal, asking him to include a preliminary paper of mine I am rather pleased with these things. But you mustn't get the idea that I am doing anything but brain anatomy these days.

I knew you would be pleased about Tischer; I did it only for your sake, for I am rather overawed by his high prices. I have so far received only one suit which I wear in the mornings (ophthalmology is clean work) and take off in the afternoons when I go to the laboratory.

This business about Dr. R., which so horrified you, is nothing bad and certainly not new. Patronage it is, but not misplaced, for he is really an able man. There is no other way of becoming an assistant professor except by a recommendation from an associate professor.

What does it matter about the cross? We are not superstitious or piously orthodox.

Are you all right again, my darling? I am in excellent health. The bit of success in my work also helps me along. Nothnagel was at the meeting today, but very impatient to get home. Either one of his children was ill or ten patients at ten florins a head were waiting for him.

I have been to see Fleischl three times, but each time he was asleep. It's impossible to get along with Meynert he doesn't listen, nor does he understand what one says. I am giving him lots of my slides, so he rather likes seeing me these days.

Goodnight, my darling, good luck to us and may our dreams come true.

Your
Sigmund

60
To Martha Bernays

Vienna, Sunday,
May 17, 1885

Precious darling

While you are taking such pleasure in the activities and management of the household, I am at the moment tempted by the desire to solve the riddle of the structure of the brain; I think brain anatomy is the only legitimate rival you have or ever will have. Let me tell you about this first: I have had some rather lucky ideas recently and enough points of view from which to go on working. I even hope here and there to draw an important conclusion from my discoveries. Yesterday I received from Berlin a very flattering letter promising to include my paper, provided I send it at once and that it doesn't run to more than a page, as promised. When the letter came I was suffering from migraine, the third attack this week, by the way, although I am otherwise in excellent health—I suspect the tartar sauce I had for lunch in Fleischl's room disagreed with me—I took some cocaine, watched the migraine vanish at once, went on writing my paper as well as a letter to Prof. Mendel, but I was so wound up that I had to go on working and writing and couldn't get to sleep before four in the morning. Today I am in fine fettle again, very pleased with my paper which is short but contains some very important information and should raise my esteem again in the eyes of the public. It is to appear either on the first or fifteenth of June, depending on whether it can still be placed or has to take its turn.

Today I missed making one important find because the slide in which I had put great hopes turned out to be useless, so now I shall have to wait for a new one. Otherwise I go on working hard.

You, Marty, why are you keeping me on tenterhooks like this? If what you want to tell no one but me concerns Elise and it is only on her account that you are all worked up and preoccupied, I am perfectly happy to wait till we have nothing more important to talk about. What could be there that you don't want to write to me about? If it is Elise's private affair, all you have to do is say so, and I won't want to hear any more about it.

If I would like to see you again? Darling, what a question! Where the money is coming from? Darling, I don't know. If it doesn't come from a very doubtful travelling grant, then I am quite willing to take a job for the summer with a rich family and visit you in the autumn with the money saved. Like last year, when I was offered a job for two hundred florins a month. That time I did turn it down, but never regretted it, for otherwise I would have missed our most successful period.

How nice of you to have remembered Paneth. I quite forgot about it. I realize that people will love me only on your account. Tischer has turned up with the second magnificent suit; I wonder if you will see it while it is still new. God only knows what I owe him already! I will pay him in installments as several colleagues in the hospital do.

The weather is lovely again today. I didn't go out, I dislike any distraction that doesn't make me forget I am alone. Going for walks makes me melancholy.

I have just finished a letter to Schonberg; now I must ask you for his address.

For our thirty fifth monthly memorial I send you fond greetings and (long to!) kiss you many times.

Your
Sigmund

61
To Martha Bernays

Vienna, Tuesday,
May 26, 1885

My precious darling

It would seem that as a result of the sympathy existing between us, your Whitsun has been no better than mine; that would be bad. Did you never wonder when you left Vienna how we should ever meet again? Don't you remember how pleased I was when you promised me to remain here? I was well aware what I should have to thank your fond relations for. As yet I see no road leading to Wandsbek this year. My American is good for only forty florins a month, if he lasts, and altogether won't produce more than 120 florins. Of this sum at least half will have to be put aside for Mother. The travelling grant wouldn't get me to you before October, but how glad I would be even of that! You know what we well do? We will just sit still and be disconnected, I think, and that's all.—I am not so fond and capable of work as I should b; perhaps lack of sleep is to blame. Whitsunday night I was at Fleischl's again, and consider the tangible benefit of such a night, the intellectual elation, the stimulation and the clarifying of so many opinions, well worth the loss of sleep. But at 4 A.M. I am afraid I feel asleep in his armchair, and when I woke at 6:30 his face showed its tenders, most suffering expression, ad he was writing a treatise. This magic world of intellect and unhappiness contributes a great deal, of course, toward estranging me from my surroundings; I have seldom felt so uncomfortable in the hospital as I do now. My work is also proceeding very slowly. I expect the paper to appear at the beginning of June.

I have unfavorable news about the travelling grant which I trust will be decided on Saturday. When I went to introduce myself to Dittel not long ago, he told me that one of my rivals, the more dangerous of the two, is going to withdraw on account of his "youth." Now my hope was that the Christian and to me hostile votes would be divided between the two other applicants, so that neither could equal my number of votes, as I am certain more than a third of the total. If one of them withdraws, then of course the other is more likely to beat me. Perhaps it wouldn't be so good if I were granted it, anyhow. The strange thing is, I have had several vivid dreams about it. Once I dreamed that I had got it, but the details were very blurred, and last night I dreamed very clearly that I was present at the announcement of the decision and learnt that the grant had been divided and "Christian" (it's not his name at all)

Dimmer had received one half. I the other, whereupon I wrote an extremely rude letter pointing out that three hundred florins might be sufficient to get me to Wandsbek but certainly not to Paris, and that I should have to borrow double this sum, in which case I prefer to withdraw! Paneth as a matter of fact has offered to prolong my stay in Paris out of his own pocket.

The Paneths have invited me to go and see them on Wednesday. Darling, darling, I wonder how you are, if you are feeling really well? For if so, we are sure to get if not silk, then at least linen bedspreads soon. Do you know that I really hate this whole trousseau business—and why? It strikes me as a very worthy object for jealousy. Understand?

Fondest greetings from

Your
Sigmund

Minna's birthday!

62
To Martha Bernays

Vienna,
June 6, 1885

My precious darling

Well, something is happening at last! Today I got the invitation for the oral exam which I am to take on Saturday the thirteenth before the board of professors. A mock exam, I think; nothing more. But the things that go with it! Top hat and gloves to be bought, and then what kind of coat am I to wear? I have to appear in a dress coat—am I to hire it or have it made? I have just been to see Tischer and ordered a frock coat, but I am not at all sure whether to stick to the order, if in that case I would have to hire a dress coat for the oral and for the trial lecture, but I also need a black coat as well; in fact I need both. How on earth is this to be solved? I am absolutely bewildered, and when I think of all the debts!

My leave has been granted, I have borrowed a traveling bag from Paneth and I have just had a letter from Obersteiner telling me that I cannot sleep there till Thursday. This will facilitate the move, as I can take my things over there in several stages. I am taking books and brain slides along.

I handed over fifty florins to Mother today. Breuer has againbehaved splendidly in the Fleischl affair. By saying only good things about him one doesn't give a proper picture of his character; one ought to emphasize the absence of so many bad things.

I would welcome the travelling grant, my darling, more than anything; I was really quite ready to renounce it when in my I had also abandoned the trip to Wandsbek; but now that I am assure of a small sum (hundred florins) for the latter purpose, I find it hard to dismiss the thought of such valuable assistance. One hundred florins is such a small sum for the visit, no matter how we economize and even if I don't give you any presents; I would hardly be able to stay ten days after deducting the train fare. What's more, my salary will have ceased, for I cannot ask for an extension of leave; I have to resign on September 1, which I do only too gladly. It is so appalling not to have any money, my darling. I cannot imagine who invented the take about women's dresses being so expensive that a man simply dare not marry! I shudder at the thought of my tailor's bill!

The events expected to take place on the next two Saturdays are bound to tide me over the probable boredom in Dobling. My paper on brain anatomy is due to appear in June 15. The anniversary of our engagement and Minna's birthday also fall in this period. Really an eventful month. If only everything goes well!

My American has paid his first twenty florins; they are lying here for you. He is going to pay once every two weeks and generally owes a tribute to my princess and my princess's sister. My only other source of income at the moment is Baron Sp., who has paid me two visits and perhaps will pay me two more this month.

One thing worries me. I am so terribly lazy I daren't think seriously what it is going to lead to. And heat on the top of it all. Marty, you will realize that I am not quite in control of things today.

Please go on writing to me at the old address.

Fondest greetings, my precious darling

Your
Sigmund

63
To Martha Bernays

Monday, Heilanstalt in Oberdobling
June 8, 1885

My sweet darling

Well, one lives and learns. Yesterday was a most amusing day; and today also seems strange and funny, although it is only 10:30. It would be easier for me to talk to you about it than describe it, but I will see what I can do. Have you ever seen this sanatorium? Do you remember the lovely park at the end of the Hirschen Strasse which continues to wards Grinding where the road curves? On a little hill in this park stands the sanatorium, which consists of the two-storied big "house" the small house, and a new building; opposite is the so-called nursing home for the chronic cases.

I arrived here yesterday at 8 A.M. with a walking stick for luggage and became a member of this very mixed community. I must describe the people in greater detail. First, there's Prof. JB., the overlord, whom I have known so far only by sight and reputation. An old gentleman, converted Jew, twisted features, a little wig and stiff walk, the result of gout or some nervous disease. He is associate professor of psychiatry, superintendent of the lunatic asylum, and was Meynert's teacher, but the pupil has elbowed the teacher out of all scientific jobs; only in medical practice has he been unable to get the better of him. He is not particularly talented, rather what is known as very shrewd, an old practitioner of most doubtful character, egotistic, completely unreliable, and in spite of being sixty-five or more, ready to indulge in any land of pleasure. He runs the sanatorium with a Dr. Obersteiner, a step-brother of Minister Haymerle. As B. had a single daughter and Obersteiner a single son, they got married and young Prof. Obersteiner, the son-in-law of B., is the man who really runs the place. Obersteiner is a friend of Breuer, Fleischl, Exner, et al., pupil of Briicke, so I have known him for quite a while. I have often been to see him to borrow the books I need for my publications. He is small, thin and insignificant, but of a very amiable disposition, extremely conscientious and decent. As a scientist he is industrious without having achieved anything outstanding, as a physician timid and modest. His wife is tall, pale, with pleasant features and an unmistakable resemblance to her father; she is in charge of the household management of the establishment, gets up early and shares in all the work. I have also seen two children. The elder, a boy, unfortunately half-paralyzed as the result of a brain disease.

At meals I also made the acquaintance of the assistant, Dr. K., who has already been here twelve years, a good-looking and terribly boring Teuton. He is married, lives in with his family; his wife looks strikingly like my niece, Pauline. Both left today. The staff consists of an inspector, an imposing fellow, a Fraulein Toni in the kitchen, and a Fraulein Marie as a companion for the ladies, both respectable, solid matrons; countless male nurses and housemaids, the latter very pretty and probably chosen by the old professor. There are sixty patients in the house, mental cases of every shade from light feeblemindedness, which the layman wouldn't detect, to the final stages of withdrawal. The medical treatment is negligible, confined to their secondary surgical and internal complaints; the rest consists of supervision, nursing, diet, and noninterference. The kitchen of course is in the [big] house. The mildest cases lunch with the director, the doctor, and the inspector. Needless to say, they are all rich people: counts, countesses, barons, etc. The *pieces de resistance* are two highnesses, Prince S. and Prince M. The latter, as you may remember, is a son of Marie Louise, wife of Napoleon, and thus, like our emperor, a grandson of Emperor Franz. You cannot imagine how dilapidated these princes and counts look, although they are not actually feeble-minded, rather a mixture of feeble-minded and eccentric.

Now for myself. I have every reason to be pleased with the reception I was given. The old professor welcomed me with great friendliness, inquired about the oral and the traveling grant, for which he held out some hope, I was alone with the professors for breakfast and coffee both yesterday and today. Oberstemer of course showed me the ropes and is as nice as he always has been. It seems that I impressed him quite a lot with, some diagnoses, and he praised my usefulness in connection with an American who arrived the day before yesterday, and my talent for remembering the names and faces of patients, although in this respect he is bound to receive some disappointments. The food is very good; there's a second breakfast at 11:30, lunch at 3 P.M. Yesterday before supper I went into town. As I am still homeless, Obersteiner has lent me his library, a cool room with views over all the hills round Vienna; there is a microscope and the walls are covered with a wealth of literature on the nervous system, which will make it hard to be bored. They have arranged a corner of B.'s salon for me to eat and write in. At the moment the table is being laid in there; I am writing this in the library. On Thursday a room will be put at my disposal where I will also have my meals alone. The working schedule is as follows: from 8:30 to 10 A.M. we make our rounds together; Obersteiner then drives to town and returns between 2 and 4 P.M.; during his absence I am in charge; once in a while there is a clinical job to be done, a young lady may have to be fed with a probang, as happened today, information given to visitors or official committees. From the morning rounds until lunch at three I am free, apart from the possibility of the above-mentioned interruptions, and then from 3 to 7 P.M. when there is another round of the sickrooms to be made. Provided one is neither the director nor the cook, there is very little to do, and one really could lead an idyllic life here with wife and child if it weren't for the lack of the challenging and stimulating element of the struggle for existence. It is actually something like a civil service job. But if things outside don't go well and I am absolutely determined to continue work on brain anatomy, I will inquire of my little woman whether such an existence, in which she wouldn't have to worry even about the kitchen, would suit her. It has its pros and cons, but I don't want to think about it now.

Apart from the idleness and the good food, I shall be able to make other uses of these three weeks: I am writing a case history and collecting the material for a new publication in connection with which some anatomical examinations will have to be made. I will also study the slides which I made last month.

Yes, write to me at this address: Dr. S. F., physician in the Oberdöbling Sanatorium, Hirschengasse 71. I want to spend as much time as possible here so that the people in return for their good treatment will also benefit from my presence. I am having my consulting hours only on Wednesdays and Fridays, when my American comes; otherwise I won't have much to do in town.

Fondest greetings to you
Your
Sigmund

64
To Martha Bernays

**Vienna, Friday
June 19, 1885**

My beloved little woman

I have been yearning for you recently more than I ever have since that first time we were forced to separate. This is the result of your sweet, tender letter, which I carry with me wherever I go. I am so boundlessly happy about it, but I realize that such complete satisfaction renders one speechless. All 1 can tell you is that had it taken not three but seven years—according to our patriarch's custom—for my courting to succeed, I would have considered it neither too early nor too late. How silly that sounds, and how annoying it is when one is accustomed to be in command of the language and all of a sudden it refuses to obey. I have always respected you highly for the very reticence of which I have so often complained: I could never trust the love that readily responds to the first call and dismisses the right to grow and unfold with time and experience—no, I just cannot find the right words. I would rather dwell on how fast the next 2/2 months are going to pass, how happy we will be with one another then and how we shall work toward keeping the time we have set ourselves, or even curtail it. Then I will tell you everything and you will understand me better than I can hope at the moment. But I do hope that you doubt my love only very rarely, only in moments of great agitation. You know, after all, how from the moment I first saw you I was determined-no, I was compelled—to woo you, and how I persisted, despite all the warnings of common sense, and how immeasurably happy I have been ever since, how 1 regained all my confidence and so on —my beloved Marty.

Life in the sanatorium is far more pleasant than I dared to expect, largely on account of Obersteiner's great, unhypocritical amiability, which springs from genuine goodness. I also get long very well with the old man; once in a while when someone comes to be treated by him, I act as his private assistant, and he has also promised to send me patients for electrical treatment. Here and there he drops a bit of advice—for instance., to concentrate on nervous diseases among children; if only one could get an official call for this!

Tomorrow, Saturday, they are not only going to report and vote on my oral as well as set me a subject and date for my trial lecture, there will also be a vote on the traveling grant, which is terribly important to me, although no longer quite so urgent as at the time when my coming to you depended exclusively on this decision.

I dream about this grant every night; yesterday, for instance, I dreamed that Brücke told me I couldn't get it, that there were seven other applicants, all of whom had greater chances!

With these two pictures our album is now full; the moment a new photograph is taken—in September—I have decided to start a new Martha album.

I greet you and Minna fondly and will soon give you further news [about the decision] and . . .

Your
Sigmund

65
To Martha Bernays

Vienna, Saturday
June 20, 1885

Princess, my little Princess

Oh, how wonderful it will be! I am coming with money and staying a long time and bringing something beautiful for you and then go on to Paris and become a great scholar and then come back to Vienna with a huge, enormous halo, and then we will soon get married, and I will cure all the incurable nervous cases and through you I shall be healthy and I will go on kissing you till you are strong and gay and happy—and "if they haven't died, they are still alive today." I wanted to send you a telegram to say that I got the traveling grant by thirteen votes to eight, but then realized you would have two whole days without any further details, and so perhaps the card will please you more. Your presentiment about the 1500 marks = 608 florins has come true. I expect a lot of good to come out of this windfall. It also goes to show that I am not unpopular with the board of professors. I am quite unspeakably happy. June really is a land month. At the same meeting my *Dozentur* was also approved, by nineteen votes to three. At the first ballot I got nineteen to one. So only two fiends joined the opposition. My trial lecture is a week from today, the twenty-seventh, on a topic connected with brain anatomy, which suits me very well.

I send you fondest greetings and just cannot get used to the idea that I am lucky, too. But did I not have the greatest bit of luck on June 17 three years ago!
With 100,000 kisses, all of which are to be cashed

Your
Sigmund

66
To Martha Bernays

Vienna, Friday,
June 26, 1885

My sweet treasure

Nothing new except your dear letter. I am brooding over my trial lecture in the most appalling heat. There are certain difficulties, for after all one does want to say something intelligent, and this is not so easy ; on the other hand , it isn't much fun slaving away for nothing and spending one's energy on things one may not be able to use. One has about twenty minutes to talk in ; if only I knew exactly how much I can pack into that time ; as it is, I am afraid what I have prepared may come to an end before my allotted time , or that from behind the folding screen of my introduction – nothing will appear. Fortunately I have already formulated the whole thing in my mind and I intend to write out this evening.

Dolfi's birthday is on July 23, three days before yours.

I do wish I could bring you the beautiful roses, my darling, which I so often find in my room. I share this favor with most of the patients. You shall be compensated when I am in Wandsbek. I do wish I could get some more money from somewhere; the two months ahead must produce something so that instead of economizing we can live as we did last year. A little happiness does everyone good, especially after so much bad luck. I must tell you something: I can feel I can hardly survive another two months; when it was six months and there was no certain prospect of our meeting, it was easier. You know, when one is traveling to America the journey as far as Stockerau passes very quickly, but from there time begins to drag. And the return journey is the same, the last but from Stockerau seems so slow. I don't want to fall into the habit of putting everything off by saying, "We will talk about this when we are together." Just remember what things were like two months ago; I had smallpox, and that was all. Now so much has changed. I even think of my stay in Döbling as a lucky episode; Breuer pointed out to me that I may owe the grant to it, as it brought me the votes of B. and his friends.

I am just about to be called to supper – till then I will keep on writing. I think after all I would prefer the room in your house, for then I will keep on writing. I think after all I would prefer the room in your house, for then I will get up early and startle you out of your sleep every morning with lots of kisses. One can love another properly only when one is close. What is a memory compared to what one can behold! –

I am wondering who will turn up at the lecture tomorrow. I haven't invited anyone. Strange to think that I shall be standing in Brucke's auditorium where I did my first work and with an enthusiasm I have never known since, and where I had hoped to stand at least as an assistant before the old man. Could this be an omen suggesting that I may after all return here for scientific work and teaching? Do you believe in omens? Since I learned that the first sight of a little girl sitting at a well-known long table talking so cleverly while peeling an apple with her delicate fingers , could disconcert me so lastingly, I have actually become quite superstitious. Do you remember, you unsuspecting worm?

If the energy I feel within me remains with me, we may yet leave behind us some traces of our complicated existence. I don't think I am ambitious, although not exactly unsusceptible to recognition. I want to have you myself, some freedom, and a few possessions; I want to keep my nervous system intact and to be left in peace by the rest of my body.

I have been reading off and on a few things by the "mad" Hoffman, mad, fantastic stuff, here and there a brilliant thought. Once, for instance, a fairy presents a bride with a necklace which has the power of preventing her from ever being annoyed about a greasy spot on her dress or a spoiled soup. Isn't that amusing?

Saturday, June 27

So now I can tell you that the trial lecture is over, too. At last! It went off quite well, only at the end something funny happened. I finished before the Dean had shouted his "Sufficit" (Enough), bowed and went off, which is against the rules; one is supposed to go on talking until interrupted by the "Sufficit". Brucke, Meynert, and Fleischl were there. My friends didn't turn up till toward the end because the Dean had made me change places with someone else. It is only from now on that I am considered a real Dozent.

I had to have lunch with Fleischl afterwards, and didn't get home till four. I will stay there another two days; on Tuesday I will be in the hospital. My interest is of course concentrated on the St. Gilgen business. I have an idea I will go, although I won't have the opportunity of doing any work, and for this reason I would rather it didn't come about. On the other hand I see clearly that I could be of some use to him. The whole story will remain undecided for several days, because on Sunday and Monday Breuer is going to join his wife in Berchtesgaden. I on the other hand am still two months away from my darling, to who go fond greetings from her.

Privatdozierenden
Sigmund

It has been frightfully hot, and I am exhausted.

67
To Martha Bernays

Vienna, Sunday,
July 5, 1985

My sweet darling

Look here, I really don't understand you at all. To be quite so good-natured as to let people get away with everything and to become incapable of taking offense really ceases to be a virtue. I am not prudish and respect you all the more for not being so, either; but how you, after all that has happened in connection with Elise, and above all after the last incident, could think of honoring her with your visit – this is beyond me. I will spare myself the sermon which you can preach to yourself, but it all reminds me so vividly of our bad times, the conditions for which I had thought were gone for good. A human being must be able to pull himself together to form a judgment, otherwise he turns into what we Viennese call a *guten Potschen*. It is just the kind of thing that almost persuaded me to leave you to Herr Fritz Wahle when he insisted he had older claims on you and you failed to find word or gesture to turn them down. *Pfui*, I don't want to think about that and what might have happened as a result and you really shouldn't do anything to remind me of it. What is the good of your feeling that you are now so mature that is relationship can't do you any harm? A girl doesn't intentionally lower herself to irresponsible behavior such as your friend has always suggested and finally quite openly displayed. I am not worrying about the question of decency, which doesn't seem to worry Elise, but about the utter weakness and lack of principle. Let her by all means be the poor girl who looks for a man, no matter where, and let us be glad she has found one. But don't put yourself on the same level by keeping up friendly relations. Don't say I'm too hard; you are far too soft, and this is something I have got to correct, for what one of us does will also be charged to the other's account. You have given me a bad day. Marty; please let me know soon that you feel a bit sorry about it. I know that with you all this springs from pity for others, must have consideration for themselves as well.

I just couldn't let all this pass without reproaching you, and I don't think I shall regret it. But, my poor sweet darling, are you so unhappy at home that you want to leave under any conditions? Please let me know what is going on. What is it that has come between us? Am I still not your confidant? Can you separate your confidence from your love? Just you wait, when I come you will soon get used to having a master again. And a severe one too, but you couldn't have one who loves you more or who could be so deeply concerned about you. This you know yourself. Oh, how I curse the wretched time till September, till I can snatch a kiss from my sweet, good little princess who is incapable of being cross which makes me cross.

Your
Sigmund

68
To Martha Bernays

Vienna, Sunday, at night,
July 5, 1985

My sweet darling

I have never written to you from this place before. I am sitting at Fleischl's desk while he is asleep next door and I don't know how long I shall be able to write. I am writing to you because I so deeply regret the angry words I wrote to you this afternoon. I don't know how you will take what I said, and that's why I am adding this. I am so terribly sorry if I said something which sounded unloving, and especially from this distance. When we are together a more serious or severe word can be followed at once by a tender reconciliation, and the little storm only testifies to the soundness of the structure. But when we are so far apart each word has time to engrave itself on one's memory, and there is no friendly hand to smooth it out. I don't know what to do. I just couldn't accept what you wanted to do without making serious objections, and yet – I realize how can one offend by love the person one loves most- and yet I am now, afterwards, inclined to let anything happen rather than have brought you to the verge of tears.

I do hope you won't take it too much to heart. You are so good, and sweet, and full of compassion and kind of interpretations, you surely won't consider the influence I am trying to exert upon you as the result of an unloving and unjust disposition. Do you remember how once, after we had parted in anger, I soon came back to you, and you said you would never forget? In the same way, I am not ashamed to come back to you now and ask once more for a kind word, a friendly glance. You are my precious little woman and even if you make a mistake you are none the less so, but you must be able to take some criticism and return it if you feel like doing so. There was a time when you did me a gross injustice and caused me great suffering and I think you really had to hear about it often enough, but believe me , it affected me more deeply than anything else in my life. But if you are in my debt I am proud of it, and if my love were not so strong I would have been less violent in my accusations and not so sensitive to the memory of them now.

If you are still keeping something from me, I promise I won't say another word about it, but please clear it up soon and don't do it again, my beloved girl. After all, it is so unnecessary to make me feel I needn't know everything that concerns you; you know this is just what I demand of you, and I do it myself. You have also often promised me to do it and I have always been so happy I have been able to think of you with absolute trust. Now we will soon be seeing another again and have a lovely time together, and then it looks as though I can expect a swift promotion and I will fetch you at the appointed time and then we will live in such unclouded happiness and undisturbed closeness, and for this time, which is soon to come, you must give me some credit and you won't be disappointed. But you know all this, my sweet child, and I am sure you are glad we are so much closer to our goal, and when in an hour of yearning you write as you did recently for our anniversary, I fall silent with joy and am so grateful to have you, but I cannot put it into words.

So what are you doing, precious Martha, my deeply loved little bride; why do you want to leave home, what can I do to make the journey possible? After all, we have money enough at the moment. Please unburden your heart to me once more. Could I possibly have become too inattentive to understand your subtly implied wishes by reporting day after day on the favorable and unfavorable things that occur to me on my way to you? Just demand what you want, just tell me, don't make me feel too how far away I am from you. Remain for me as fresh and gay as I can only imagine you to be; we will survive this slice of time, too – and then I will never write to you again, nothing good and nothing bad, for I will never leave you till I realize I have become a bit too much for you, and then I will go away and wait and see if you will call me back.

Your devoted

Sigmund

69
To Martha Bernays

Meidling, 12:45 PM,
July 23, 1885

My little princess

Your card received early this morning; I am so sorry I didn't understand your Hamburgese. Very sweet of you to send me the five marks, girl; why are we already anticipating the bad times? Please send me a financial report. For your information, I already have a trunk and a traveling bag; Moritz has left both with me.

Now to explain the situation. We – Dolfi and I, of course- are lunching are on our great Semmering excursion. At 1:30 we are taking the train to Payerbach, then we walk part of the way, spend the night somewhere and return early tomorrow morning. Quite an experience for the little one.

Semmering, 10 P.M.

Everything has gone very well, most glorious weather, excellent butter, honey and a quarter *Gespritzer*, everything at its best. Having thought at the outset that any pleasure without you must be a torture, I ended up by enjoying it myself. We took the road from Klamm into the Adlizgräben, then on to Semmering. In the Adlizgräben, then on to Semmering. In the Adlizgräben we came upon a charmingly situated Gasthaus with a dear, tiny little waitress, and Dolfi, with her common sense, suggested spending the night there. But I insisted on going on to the Archduke Johann on the Styrian border.

Now come the adventures. We arrive there; despite hints I fail to ask if we may spend the night. We take another walk, return late- and they won't have us. Now by faint moonlight over the mountain to the hotel, then to the tourist house, to the diary, no room anywhere; we inquire the way to the Gasthaus but they refuse to believe we can find it in the dark. Finally the innkeeper consents to make up some beds in his little dining room, and here we are eating our supper in peace. Dolfi is holding out very well, she marches like an old soldier, has no fear of "dark forests", is continually gay and happy and doesn't reproach me in the least although she has every reason for doing so. I have given free play to all the fountains of my irresponsibility: I haven't even brought enough money along, and she has to help me out! I know how you would scold me under these circumstances, but in that case I could kiss you, and then I would have deserved it. I really have arranged things very stupidly, but I am enjoying myself very much all the same. Oh, if only I had you with me, my sweet princess! I will really have to pull myself together during the next forty days and reduce my careless way of living. I can understand very well why you don't like my counting the days. I wanted to give my poor little sister a nice birthday and this has been a success. But from now on till I see you there will be only serious , hard-working , and thrifty days so as to feel I have earned my luck.

I tore the sheet of notepaper I brought along in two, gave one half to Dolfi, and am writing this on a scrap of paper I happened to have on me. We return tomorrow morning; I want to spend your birthday in solitary contemplation.

Good night, my little woman

Your
Sigmund

70
To Martha Bernays

Vienna, Wednesday,
August 5, 1885

My precious darling

You too are surprised at Schonberg's traveling plans, aren't you? As a matter of fact he isn't here; please have a look at the card and see whether he says the "middle of next month" or "week". Perhaps it is just a slip of the pen. Yes, we shall be very happy in Wandsbek; anyway for me Wandsbek is not what it is for you. More like what Vienna is for me.

I must give you a report on last night's jollification with our chief. It was very genial, particularly in his company; only on our way home we had to admit that the evening had left a bad taste in our mouths. But from this kind of remark one doesn't learn much; I must describe it to you in detail. Well, he – do you know L.?

I will tell you his history. Once upon a time there lived in Pressburg a certain Moritz L. (certainly not the only one of that name), a man as poor as only a Jew can be. Or rather, his father was as poor as that; I am not sure whether he was a peddler or a *schammes* or a dealer in secondhand clothes, I think the second of the three. But this didn't prevent the young Moritz from attending Pressburg grammar school, and there it transpired that he had come into the world with a so-called Jewish brain. At school he was almost invariably top, very industrious, although he had to spend most of his time giving private lessons; a typical little Jew with sly features, a boundless vivaciousness and the gift of the gab, otherwise quite an honest fellow. Needless to say, Moritz L. had to go to Vienna to study medicine; there he suffered months and years of starvation, finally became a tutor and as a result could take his doctor's degree in peace. Then he joined the hospital, for a while he was assistant physician at Loew's sanatorium, and there he made the acquaintance of the professors. The day came for him to be made *Sekundarazt* and his application got him the position with J., which was more or less the same as being his assistant. At this time J. was writing his great work and needed a stenographer, for which he employed his *Sekundarazt* who before long became a collaborator. Thus, Dr. Moritz L. grew to be an intimate of the J. household, in which considerable brutality and crudeness existed, but also a beautiful daughter by the name of Marthe. Suddenly he became J.'s son-in-law; rumor had it that this was considered necessary because the child of the Viennese professor had grown too fond of the intelligent Jewish boy. But there is no need to believe this- or, if one does, to assume any evil intention on the part of either. In short, L., son of the *Schammes* , turned in to L. the *Dozent,* associate professor , and finally , since 1881 , J.'s successor , who by the way is very fond of his wife and invited us only because she is in the country and he was feeling lonely.

And there he sat, the same man despite his forty-eight years, the same sly features and incessant talk. We were his guests: old Dr. Ricchetti. Lustgarten and I, the two *Aspirants* and an American who has been attached to the clinic for a long time. He treated us to fish, poultry, cheese, beer, wine, champagne, and cigars and never for a moment stopped talking, mostly about himself; as a true parvenu he indulged in memories of his poverty-stricken youth when one coffee a day was all he had to sustain him; he revealed the whole series of lucky incidents to which he owed his rise to the position of J.'s assistant; he was very full of himself and very happy. The atmosphere was unrestrained, for the character of this vain, rather transparent man has aspects which one cannot help respecting, among them the lack of any trace of pompousness and conceit, no shame at being a Jew. There isn't very much to be said against him except that he seems to consider he has fulfilled his task in life by having been so fortunate. Since becoming a professor he hasn't made a worthwhile contribution, and instead of assuming the leadership in the field, he lets everything pass him by and amuses himself by cultivating the role of a worldly-wise, rather senile observer.

That in spite of all my moderation the banquet has not contributed to making me feel any better is, I suppose, to be expected. Yesterday and today have been bad days despite Karlsbad salts and a cold bath. The truth is, my energy has been spent again; every inch of me is longing to be happy with you, to kiss you, and to be compensated for this endlessly long year.

Please thank Minna warmly for her friendly letter; I am too lazy and feel too disagreeable to answer now. But don't you worry, I will revive as though touched by a magic wand the moment I am with you, and then everything will be so beautiful.

Fondest greetings and kisses
Your Sigmund

71
To Martha Bernays

Vienna, Thursday,
August 6, 1885

My lovable little woman

I have just got back from Baden. As you have seen him [Schönberg] recently I won't describe to you what he looks like now – without flesh or blood, without voice or breath. One of his lungs is completely destroyed, and the other probably riddled with disease. I consider him a lost man ; how fast or how slowly the miserable remains will take to burn themselves out, I don't know ; in Vienna he would probably last three months, what could be achieved by a better climate, care , and quiet remains to be seen.

For us in any case he is lost. His wretched soul is weary; enthusiasm for an aim, passion, and the halo with which one surrounds the woman of one's choice, all these are the products of health. When the breath comes short, interest narrows , the hear abandons all desire, nothing remains but a tired , resigned philosopher ; he has found his way back to the once despised family , is incapable of holding anything against them , grateful for any attention they show him, and above all is in need of peace , only peace. What a lot there would have been to talk about in the past if one of us had seen our girls! When I broached the subject, he said: "You agree, don't you, with my having broken off the engagement?" I then began repeating to him what I had written to Minna : that the breaking off is not important since their feelings remain the same and that otherwise they were dependent on circumstances over which they had no control ; but he said "no", and I suddenly realized I was wrong and that his love had died before him. What has brought him to the point of renouncing everything he has clung to for so long – work and position, independence from his brother, and his own willfulness – I don't know. Is this the end of a long, hard struggle or a symptom of the psyche going to sleep? He had difficulty in speaking, and said little of importance beyond warding off my anger with his family.

Tomorrow or Tuesday I will go out and see him with Dr. Müller. For I have made it quite clear to him that I am acting simply as his friend and have also told Geza a few bitter truths, but that chap is too stupid and conceited. As a matter of fact they now seem to realize he is in need of being taken care of and agree to everything, the silly fools.

Schönberg let one word slip out which hurt me very much. He told me how good Martha had been to him and she looked well but had "dark rings under her eyes" – Why has my little woman dark rings under her eyes? From that moment my spirits fell and all the selfishness of a human being revealed itself by my being much more shaken by your dark rings than by the poor man's deplorable condition.

When I come I am going to fatten you up and kiss some color into your cheeks; and just you wait, I am not going to allow myself to be sent away on October first.

Your
Sigmund

72
To Martha Bernays

Vienna, Wednesday,
August 12, 1885

My wandering princess

Fancy, Lübeck! Should that be allowed? Two single girls traveling alone in North Germany! This is a revolt against the male prerogative, the beginning of the realization that one doesn't have to be lonely without a man. Haven't you had any adventures? I would rather have enjoyed that. So there is nothing left for me to do but express my pleasure that you got along so well in Lübeck, which I do herewith.

You won't expect any great change in my circumstances since last night, but something new I can report is that I received a summons to appear tomorrow at the police station; but don't be alarmed, it is obviously connected with my *Dozentur*. The government wants to know where I haven't some vile deed to confess that would render me unworthy of the noble title. I am determined not to divulge a thing.

Eliot's *Middlemarch* in four volumes is lying in front of me, and my handkerchiefs are coming to an end, but no so my cold. Any now I am off to luncheon and when I get back I will report on my financial misery.

I have to tell you about it because to my own deep regret I must reveal the fact that I won't be able to bring you any present , something I had been looking forward to so much , probably more than you. So listen. I have asked Paneth to send me three hundred florins, and I intend to borrow a further ninety from Breuer, which will bring my debt to him to fifteen hundred. Now, this is to be distributed as follows: one hundred florins to Tischer, the first and probably the only installment for a long time to come l two hundred florins for September in Wandsbek, journey included, rather too little than too much, for last year we went through more than that and still had to economize toward the end. This leaves only one hundred and seventy for my stay. Now, of the ninety florins from Breuer, seventy-five goes to the bookseller, seven to the shoemaker, five to the French teacher (I have decided to take only five more lessons). Trunk, box, and packer – will thirty florins be too much for all this? (A hat – but no, there will be time for that in Hamburg.) My chairwoman, five to eight florins; in short, I realize I shall be very lucky if I am left with twenty florins, of which something must go to those at home. If I am left with thirty, which would pay for the journey, then I would bring a full two hundred florins to Wandsbek, which is what I would like to do. Remember, we won't be getting another penny before October 1. Thus there won't be anything left for you, my darling; I feel the loss of the forty florins caused by the departure of my last patient. That I won't be able to bring you anything I have foreseen ever since then, and it doesn't contribute to raising my spirits, for I would love to have given myself this pleasure. May I point out that if I leave on the thirtieth, there are still eighteen days to be endured? A long and difficult time, and one not likely to make me feel any better.

Let us take some French lessons in Wandsbek; can you find a decent and not too expensive teacher? Life is so full of little worries.

Fondest Greetings

**Your
Sigmund**

73
To Martha Bernays

Vienna, Friday,
August 14, 1885

My precious little woman

I went to Baden yesterday afternoon and didn't get back till this morning. Astonishing how much better he [Schönberg] looks; most of the symptoms have subsided; I don't think the end will come for some time. He is so satisfied with the way his brother and sister-in-law are looking after him that I too find myself reconciled to this couple. In conversation the brother tried to clear himself of all responsibility for the neglect, and in fact it turns out that it was mainly because Schönberg's irritability while here, his permanent secretiveness and his protestations about his improving health while in England, that the family didn't make it their business to look after his health before. We went to the theater in the Baden Arena, to a box where one could smoke! – And during the performance of *The Beggar Student*, I questioned him much as a father confessor questions his penitent.

I spent the night with Schönberg to give him a chance of confiding in me once more; he has a beautiful room in the Frauenhof, and we talked for a long time before going to sleep. I asked him outright why, when we sounded the alarm, he put up such a resistance against coming here. His answer seemed to be sincere. For diplomatic reasons, he said. At that time he wasn't ill enough to expect any help from his family and was afraid that if he came here of his own accord he would again be without any financial support he added that he had the greatest difficulties in obtaining the money for the journey to Oxford. When it comes to guilt, human beings seem to be quite willing to share!

I also asked him if he had any particular wish, and he answered that his greatest, indeed his only wish at the moment was to know for certain that his engagement to Minna had been broken off. He said he had informed his brother that he had been engaged but that he wasn't any longer, because he had felt an overwhelming desire to establish in the presence of one person that he is not engaged. He added that he felt an actual aversion to Minna, hoped her vivacious temperament would soon help her to forget him and that she will behave as an unattached girl; I promised to do everything to make things easy for him. 'Don't you think that the psychic burden of such a relationship is too great for me? My egotism is beginning to assert itself. All I really want is to keep going for a few years." The poor man, I told him that of course the dislike he had taken to everything was the result of his exhaustion. During the evening, after he had bowed to a lady, his sister-in-law remarked: "It's also a sign of improvement that he is beginning to be more polite to women again." I leave it to your judgment, which in Schönberg's case has always turned out to be so correct, how much of this you will feel passing on to Minna. The final prognosis of his condition remains the same, in spite of the present improvement.

In the evening I kept thinking that if serious illness made it impossible for us to marry, we two would behave differently. I have been looking upon you for a long time as my own, and I would never set you free ; I would accept the fact that you suffered with and about me, and I doubt that you , my little woman , would do otherwise. A human being is so miserable when all he wants is to stay alive.

I am going to see Hammerschlag tomorrow morning , spend the night there, and on Sunday go on to Herzig. I am delighted to hear the news from Segeberg.

Fondest greetings from

Your
Sigmund

74
To Martha Bernays

Paris
October 19, 1885

My beloved darling

My lazy life could have come to an end today. I went to the Salpêtrière, which is just as big and has as many courtyards as our hospital, to introduce myself to the medical assistant and ask when Charcot[1] is expected. The assistant, however, was not there; he has already been replaced by a new one, and Charcot was in the wards. I could have gone in there, but I had left rny introduction at home, and so this step upon which so much depends has to wait till tomorrow. The *Consultation Externe—i.e.,* the consultation for outpatients—takes place at 9:30. So perhaps by tomorrow 1 shall already be occupied with work. The lectures at the École de Medecine don't begin till November 5, but if things with Charcot work out well I shall hardly have much to do there. The medical library is on the first floor of the École de Medecine; it contains a great number of magazines, including German and English ones, and here I shall probably spend many an hour.

One of Charcot's books, which I already own in the German translation, I have now bought for four francs so as to learn French from the translation- My laziness is beginning to worry me terribly; for days now my sense of guilt has not allowed me one calm hour. Apart from some subjective and scientific profit, I expect so little from my stay here that in this respect I cannot be disappointed.

I can barely remember what J did yesterday. My evening at the theater on the seventeenth gave me migraine. Believe it or not, performances here last from eight till midnight! and the heat is appalling. J went with John; the lowest (i.e., highest) seat costs one franc; we paid 1.50, *quatrieme loge de cdte,* really disgraceful pigeonhole boxes, in a corner of the highest balcony, where one is aware of being alone, but not much more, Just think of our evening in the theater in Hamburg! I was struck by the total absence of elegant dresses; I suppose they keep these for the Opera. There is no music, no orchestra, and the signal for the play to begin consists of three blows with a hammer behind the curtain. The plays were *Le Manage Force, Tartuffe* and *Les Precieuses Ridicules,* all by Moliere, and although I couldn't understand a word of what the women, and only half of what the men said, I enjoyed enormously the brilliant acting. *Tartuffe* I knew, of course, and what was remarkable about the last play was not so much the dialogue as the high comedy of the two Coquelins. During

Tartuffe the audience applauded every speech of any length. My migraine is rather discouraging me from frequent visits to the theater; I really went in the hope of learning French, for I have no one to talk to and every day I seem to get worse at uttering these wretched sounds. I don't think I am mistaken if I say already that I shall never achieve a tolerable "accent," but it must at least be possible to construct a sentence correctly.

The walk I took three days ago, of which I owe you a description, led along the Quai d'Orsay, where the ministries are, past the Dome des Invalides, across the Seine and on to the Avenue des Champs Elysees., the most stylish part of Paris, as John would say; here there are no shops at all and people travel only by horse and carriage. Elegant ladies walk here with expressions suggesting that they deny the existence in this world of anyone but themselves and their husbands or are at least graciously trying to ignore it; one side of the avenue is formed by an extensive park in which the prettiest children spin their tops, ride on merry-go-rounds, watch the Punch-fit-Judy show, or drive themselves about in little carriages drawn by goats. On the benches sit wet nurses feeding their babies, and nursemaids to whom the children dash screaming after they have had a quarrel. I couldn't help thinking of poor Mitzi and grew very, very furious and full of revolutionary thoughts. Walking on, one comes to the Place de la Concorde, in the center of which stands a real obelisk from Luxor. Imagine, a genuine obelisk, scribbled all over with the most beautiful birds' heads, little seated men and other hieroglyphs, at least 3000 years older than the vulgar crowd around it, built in honor of a king whose name today only a few people can read and who, but for this monument, might be forgotten! The Place de la Concorde leads into the Tuileries Gardens, which you can think of as being very nice the square between the two *Burgtoren* in Vienna (including the *Volksgarten* and both museums). Then comes the Louvre. Now I remember, of course—yesterday I went to the Louvre, at least to the antiquities wing, which contains an incredible number of Greek and Roman statues, gravestones, inscriptions, and relics. I saw a few wonderful things, ancient gods represented over and over again, as well as the famous armless Venus de Milo to whom I paid the traditional compliment. I remember that old Mendelssohn (the father in *The Famify* M.) reported on it from Paris as a new acquisition without any great show of enthusiasm. I believe the beauty of the statue was not discovered till later, and that it has become fashionable to think so. For me these things have more historical than aesthetic interest. What attracted me most was the large number of emperors' busts, some of them excellent characterizations. Most of them are represented several times and don't look in the least alike. Many of them must have been produced in factories according to the prevailing fashion. I just had time for a fleeting glance at the Assyrian and, Egyptian rooms, which I must visit again several times. There were

Assyrian longs —tall as trees and holding lions for lapdogs in their arms, winged human animals with beautifully dressed hair, cuneiform inscriptions as clear as if they had been done yesterday, and then Egyptian bas-reliefs decorated in fiery colors, veritable colossi of kings, real sphinxes, a dreamlike world.

Today I walked in an arc similar to that of three days ago, but away from the Seine and off the map which I sent you the day be' fore yesterday. I found myself surrounded by the most frantic Paris hubbub until I worked my way through to the well-known Boulevards and the Rue Richelieu. On the Place de la Republique I saw the gigantic statue with the pictorial presentations of the years 1789, 1792, 1830, 1848, and 1870. This gives some idea of the poor Republic's interrupted existence. Yesterday the bye-elections took place in France (and Paris); all the Republicans got together, for as a result of the split between the Opportunists and the Radicals., almost only Monarchists got in at the first election. The yelling of the newspaper vendors was deafening; some papers appeared in four and five editions, and I myself bought two copies. Needless to say, these bye-elections are now Republican.

Do you like the way I write from Paris? It strikes me that with all the news and descriptions I hardly ever have time for anything personal.

It is now a week since I saw you, and every day I still think I am going to see you. Again I can hardly imagine what you look like! Would it have been better for me to have gone to Berlin? I could have left there every Saturday evening and spent Sundays with you. The great benefit of my stay in Wandsbek, the physical fitness and mental calm, are still with me, but I can't really enjoy myself; I am too much in love and feel too much out of place.

News in brief; the coffee here is delicious everywhere, and the children wear the same kind of blouses as yours from San Francisco. Just think, for three toilet articles (some talcum, tar, and mouthwash) I had to pay 3.50 francs. And then one is expected to economize!

You don't mention the tooth trouble. Please tell me everything. Your last letter was not even signed; but it was from you all right, for who else would write to me so affectionately?

Your devoted
Sigmund

75
To Martha Bernays

Paris
October 21, 1885

My beloved treasure

Your letters know how to find me by now, so I here is no need for a more precise address. . . .

Today you may miss the note of melancholy to which you will have grown accustomed in my letters from Paris. The reason is that I spent yesterday and today in the Salpetriere, where everything went off better than I had expected. I am already in the midst of work and full of hope. For a deposit of three francs I was given the key of a closet in the laboratory and a *tablier* (apron) by the hospital administration. On the receipt I am described as "M. Freud, École de Medecine." Let me tell you about it in detail. When I arrived in the Salpetriere yesterday morning the *Consultation Externe—i.e.,* for outpatients—was being held. In one room sat the patients, in the other, a small one, several guest doctors, the internes, and the *Chef de Clinique* M. Marie, who examined the patients as they were admitted one at a time. At ten o'clock M. Char-cot arrived, a tall man of fifty-eight, wearing a top hat, with dark, strangely soft eyes (or rather, one is; the other is expressionless and has an inward cast), long wisps of hair stuck behind his ears., clean shaven, very expressive features with full protruding lips—in short, like a worldly priest from whom one expects a ready wit and an appreciation of good living. He sat down and began examining the patients. I was very much impressed by his brilliant diagnosis and the lively interest he took in everything, so unlike what we are accustomed to from our great men with their veneer of distinguished superficiality. I gave my card to the *Chef* who handed it to Char-cot. The latter fingered it for a while and after the consultation asked where I was. I came forward and gave him my introduction. He recognized Benedikt's handwriting, stepped aside to read it, said "Charrne de vous voir," and invited me to accompany him. He advised me to make my working arrangements with the *Chef de Clinique,* and without any further ado I was accepted. He then proceeded to show me everything in the laboratory and the lecture hall, passed through several wards and explained a great many things to me. In short, although fewer formalities were exchanged than I had expected, I soon felt very much at ease, and I realized that in the most inconspicuous fashion he was showing me a great deal of consideration. I asked his permission to show him some of my slides, which I did briefly today.

Today was the day for the ophthalmological consultations. The clinic has its own ophthalmologist, whose consulting room is as accessible to me as everything else. Altogether the atmosphere is very informal and democratic. Charcot lets fall quite casually any number of the most brilliant remarks, is constantly asking questions and always good enough to correct my wretched French. As long as he is present I try to keep near him, and already feel quite at home. The *Chef* Marie is an excellent fellow and my only regret is that he is leaving in ten clays. His successor hasn't yet arrived. Without a moment's hesitation Marie gave me the material I need for my self-chosen work (have you ever heard of secondary degeneration?), and today Charcot wrote a letter to another professor to get me some children's brains. The morning is devoted to patients, the afternoon to study. So I have good reason to be satisfied. Today I went to the clinic in the afternoon as well. The people here are not very busy yet; lectures haven't even started. The evenings I intend to spend reading in the library or studying at home, as I did today. I don't think I shall see the boys so soon again. I am completely happy to be back at work.

My new shoes arrived today, with laces and English soles, but twenty-two francs! Altogether, you would hardly believe the amount of money one needs for the most ordinary things, and how poor I am already! Needless to say, I have already written to Paneth. But my stay here is going to be well worth it, this I can see clearly. If I didn't have to think of the misery at home, I would feel quite all right. But I am so old and so weak or so wicked that I cannot deny myself a thing. I eat my fill and I smoke and I cannot do anything but—be sorry. Whenever I think of them it upsets me, but this doesn't do them any good.

You, my darling, do write as much as possible about yourself. Couldn't I for once have you and the work at the same time?

With many kisses

Your
Sigmund

76
To Martha Bernays

Paris, Wednesday
November 4, 1885

My beloved darling

Well, the great news is that yesterday on arriving rather late at the *Consultation Externe* (I am getting lazy and easygoing these days), I noticed in the audience a narrow, pale skull covered with thin, fair hair which nodded to me in recognition and which turned out to be that of my friend *in cerebro* Darkschewitsch from Moscow. Let me tell you the previous history of our relationship: when I entered Meynert's laboratory to do research on the gold method, I found there an American, Mr. Barney Sachs, a particularly amiable and intelligent man (I learned later that he is a Jew), and my Russian Darkschewitsch. The latter attracted my attention by his melancholy disposition, typical of Ruthenians and Little Russians, but I got to know him better only after I had discovered my Method. Sachs translated rny paper into English for *Brain,* or rather he corrected my translation, and D. offered to translate it for a Russian journal, which he did. He slowly began to confide in me and I discovered in him a quiet and profound fanatic. He was averse to all distractions and his soul was absorbed in the motherland, religion, and brain anatomy. His ambition was to write the first book on brain anatomy in the Russian language. Dissatisfied with Meynert, he went to Leipzig, to my rival Flechsig. He wrote to me once from there, but I never got an answer to my reply. Since March, 1884—when he left Vienna—I have read several interesting papers by him on brain anatomy. So now he is here, to spend his last year abroad in Charcot's clinic. His government has promised him a professorship on his return. After the consultation he came over to me and gave me his address; I accompanied him at once and found him unchanged and in his own quiet way very friendly. He still remembered my engagement, inquired after the health of my fiancee and expressed the hope that I won't have to keep her waiting much longer. He had also once met my father in Vienna and asked how he was. I liked all this very much and in the evening called for him, we dined together, then drank tea in his room, and I began to feel less isolated. In one paper he showed me he mentions that my Method had given Mm by far the best illustrations for his investigation, and his drawings are copied from these slides. He told me my Method had created a sensation in Leipzig, which I was glad to hear. He described Flechsig to me as an insignificant man who doesn't know how to make proper use of his own discovery. When I referred jokingly to his melancholia, it turned out that he is just as much in love as I am and waiting for letters in die very same way, and this brought us that much closer. As he is not looking for any form of social life or pleasure, he is just the right kind of company for me. On Sunday we have decided to go to Versailles together. Of course I am not indifferent to the news of the effect my minor scientific achievements are having on others. His book is well advanced; with his Russian diligence and great sobriety, he works very hard. I am very pleased to have met him.

Fondest greetings and kisses.

Your
Sigmund

77
To Martha Bernays

Paris
November 8, 1885

My beloved darling

Dimly aware that I have not written to you for ages and reminded by a card from you that by now you may have once more got used to Mama and would like to hear from me, I am writing to you again. All kinds of minor things have happened, but the most important fact for me is that my work is now proceeding smoothly and I am just reaching the proper pitch of enthusiasm, which is another reason why I haven't written. But I haven't made any discoveries as yet.

Yesterday my failure to write had another cause. My head was reeling; I had been to the Porte St. Martin theater to see Sarah Bernhardt. I am still rather tired and ravaged by the heat and the blood-&-thunder melodrama, which lasted from 8 to 12:30, but it was worth it. How shall I begin to tell you about it? I am so clumsy today at arranging things. First the minor details. We (I was with one of my Russians) paid four francs and for this were given seats in the *stalles d'orchestre,* which I suggest should be translated simply as the orchestra stable. One could see and hear perfectly., but I think I will have more room and be more comfortable in my grave; at least I will be stretched out. The play started at 8 P.M., had five acts or eight scenes (*Theodora,* of course); after the first act the excruciating heat gradually increased until toward the end it was neither describable nor bearable. And on top of that the wretched megalomania of the French for insisting on 4Ja hours of theater as they do on five- or six-course meals. To enjoy one's way through something quickly, allowing interest to help conquer fatigue, is too plebeian for them; so they prolong a 2/2-hour play by two hours of entr'acte during which one can, it's true, go out into the beautiful evening and drink beer, smoke a cigar and eat oranges; but if one returns too early (as one invariably does), one suffers the ghastly tortures of anticipation in the oven. I really cannot praise the play, Victorien Sardou's *Theodora* (he has already written a *Dora* and a *Feodora* and is said to be busy on a *Thermidora, Ecuadora,* and *Toiveadora!*}. A pompous trifle, magnificent Byzantine palaces and costumes, a conflagration, pageants of armed warriors and so on., but hardly a word anyone would want to commit to memory, and as for characterization, it leaves one completely cold. Theodora herself, Justinian's famous empress, originally a ballet dancer who, as history has found worth noting, once appeared in public *toute nue,* is in this play simply a *femme qui aime.* The French love such simplifications —think of *Donna Sol.* Theodora is deeply in love with a young patrician who has ideals and republican sympathies; her whole complicated early Me, which needless to say her lover throws in her face at the end, has to be imagined; it is certainly not shown in her behavior. But how this Sarah can act! After the first words uttered in an intimate, endearing voice, I felt I had known her all my life. I have never seen an actress who surprised me so little; I at once believed everything about her. She was almost never off the stage. In the first scene she is seen giving audience lying on a "throne sofa" with a bored, arrogant expression and receiving back in favor the disgraced Belisar. In the second scene she visits in disguise her wet nurse, who is a keeper in the circus menagerie; she plays with a tiger concealed behind some straw and seems to be rather enjoying life while helping to peel onions and sharing the nurse's meal. In the third scene, this time disguised as Myrtha, she visits her lover in his garden; in the fourth she has a little squabble with her husband, the emperor, a stiff and cowardly tyrant whom she reproaches for being a bigger hypocrite than herself. From now on the play moves a little faster; the lover and a friend enter the palace at night with intent to murder the emperor. Theodora however slams the door behind the friend, thus helping her Andreas to make his escape, and when the conspirator is caught and about to be tortured to make him divulge the name of his accomplice, she begs for a chance to speak to him, reveals to him her relationship with Andreas and orders him to think of a means of preventing him from talking under torture. He can think of only one: she has to kill him and, with the threat that he will otherwise tell the whole story, he forces her to pierce his heart (having first of all shown her the precise spot) with a golden pin which she wears in her hair. In Scene V she again visits her lover, who is in the midst of celebrating the funeral rites of his dead friend and who swears to wreak the most terrible vengeance on the murderess, Theodora. In Scene VI the emperor and empress are about to enter their box in the circus to watch the games when a man shoves his way through the crowd and yells an insult at her, whereupon he is seized and commanded to kneel in front of her before being executed. Needless to say, the man is Andreas, Pleading for him to be spared, she casts her wrap over the shackled prisoner. In Scene VII we see Justinian in the palace waiting in fear and trembling for the outcome of the battle which has broken out in the town. Andreas has made his escape and organized a rebellion. But Belisar wins, the prisoners are brought in, the gates are thrown open, and the town is seen in flames. The emperor has grown suspicious of Theodora, who is being told by her wet nurse that Andreas is lying wounded in the circus. In Scene VIII she visits him there, is compelled to listen to his reproaches and contempt and offers him a magic potion

205

which the wet nurse has brought her to make Justinian submit to her will. The potion, however, is poison, the wet nurse's son has been executed by the emperor, and this was to have been her revenge; Andreas dies and while Theodora is mourning him several courtiers appear and present themselves with a silent bow. "Ah, je comprend," she says, glancing up. "L'empereur—le bour-reau!" And then: "De quelle maniere?" The hangman shows her a silk noose, she frees her neck, says "Now I'm ready to die!" and is throttled.

I have never seen a funnier figure than Sarah Bernhardt in Scene II, where she appears in a simple dress, I am really not exaggerating. And yet one was soon compelled to stop laughing, for every inch of this little figure was alive and bewitching. As for her caressing and pleading and embracing, the postures she assumes, the way she wraps herself round a man, the way she acts with every limb, every joint—it's incredible. A remarkable creature, and I can well imagine she is no different in life from what she is on the stage. For the sake of historical truth let us add that I again had to pay for this pleasure with an attack of migraine, and so have decided to go to the theater only rarely and to pay not less than five or six francs for a seat.

The Russian I went with was Dr. Klikowicz, Botkin's assistant, a vivacious, shrewd, and amiable young man to whom I owe several practical hints. He pointed out to me a *cremerie* where one can get for thirty centimes what costs sixty in a cafe and took me to a new restaurant where one can eat *a prix fixe* and yet choose one's dishes, get twice as much to drink and more to eat than at Duval's, and yet pay twenty centimes less per meal. I would save more if I drank wine instead of beer, would pay 1.60 francs instead of 2.00. Today, Sunday, an excursion to Versailles had been planned, but I have decided to give my head and my pocket a rest.

I hope to go to several lectures with my other Russian, the "scientific" one, who has invited me to tea this evening. On Friday we actually went to one given by M. Hallopeau, a young *Dozent,* where we got a glimpse of a French amphitheater, etc. I introduced myself to the gentleman, but there is no question of being received; all one hears is "charme" (which is not true), then "I have been in Vienna, too, and made the acquaintance of Herr So-&-So.," and in future I shall go where I want and save my cards. Other foreigners I have met here feel the same as I do about the so-called civility of the French.

That is enough of this chronicle. I must add that I had a very nice letter from Dolfi. Now that I have finished my report I will write to you again more affectionately and on more personal topics and hope meanwhile to hear from you at some length.

Fond greetings from
Your ever devoted
Sigmund

78

To Martha Bernays

Paris, Thursday
November 19, 1885

My lovely darling

You are so superhumanly good I really don't know how to thank you. There are things that are tied to geography, and because of the distance between Paris and Hamburg I cannot take you in my arms and kiss you as I would like to. The newspaper was an incomparable treat for me, especially the Viennese sections with the delightful passage by Spitzer. My description is altogether most one-sided and should be taken with a grain of salt because I always try to speak the truth as far as I can and dare!

You are right, my darling, in saying that I have even more to tell you than before, and usually there is something I even forget to tell you, for instance my visit to Notre Dame de Paris on Sunday. My first impression on entering was a sensation I have never had before; "This is a church." And I looked about for Ricchetti, who knows the churches of Italy. There he stood, deeply lost in wonder. I have never seen anything so movingly serious and somber, quite unadorned and very narrow, which is no doubt partly responsible for the general impression, I really must read Victor Hugo's novel[3] here, for this is the place properly to understand it.

I hope you feel reassured about the overcoat; as a matter of fact, the cold has abated and we are having the most beautiful autumn weather. The anatomical work is very hard going; I am resigning myself more and more to my inability to work out the many stimulating ideas. Today Charcot gave me permission to embark on the clinical study for which I had an inspiration; but it looks as though Marie wants to withdraw, so I don't know what I shall be able to do. Probably nothing, but subtract all this and there is still enough to make my stay here valuable.

It is not very nice of you to lay so much stress on Frau Ricchetti's ugliness. You know well enough that however beautiful she might be, she could not be compared to Martha. In any case she is an exceptionally distinguished and nice woman, speaks four languages fluently, has read a great deal, doesn't boast about it, but rather irritates one by asking too many questions. She is very quiet when the men are talking but takes an interest in everything, is kindness itself toward her husband who cannot do without a certain amount of selfish comfort, with the result that he is always saying to me: "There's only one Louise." She allows herself to be sent wherever he wants her to go, stays with him when he wants her to, looks after him and enjoys things with him. I play a bit of the cavalier toward her, and she repays me with little attentions such as producing some doughnuts the day after I complained about the lack of dessert. She is fat, an indefatigable walker and usually walks alone. Her genealogy is as follows: she comes from Frankfurt, of a very rich family, but was herself not rich. The great Behrend in Manchester is her uncle; her dowry was sufficient for them to have lived on it very carefully, but only a few years ago she inherited a lot of money, so she is now worth some 340,000 francs. Since that time they have kept their accounts separate; he says he doesn't want to be rich through her. His own fortune, earned from his practice, amounts to 250,000 francs. But they both live so frugally that on this money they are very well off. They make no effort to cultivate friends. Our relationship consists in his taking me to the Salpetriere in the mornings, then we return to his house, pick up his wife, and go to Duval's. In the afternoon I return alone, come back to them at six, at seven o'clock we go out to dine, and then go for a walk or I spend another hour with them in their apartment.

I do wish we were already in the position to accept the invitation to stay with them in the Palazzo Buffo in Venice. You would get along splendidly with these two excellent people. By the way, she used to know Michael Bernays in Frankfurt—thirty-eight years ago. She was a bit confused about the time and asked if you are a sister of his, but soon realized you must be a niece.

Today I had a letter from Paneth and an interesting paper by him. So much news that there's hardly a chance for an affectionate word. My precious, beloved darling, when I think that you are my bride and have been so for 3J£ years, I see myself in turn as worthy of envy and pity. Like the wind, you say? It is half the engagement time of our patriarchs, but they lived to an incredible age and God was on their side. Fare thee very well and thank you again for yoirr amusing enclosures.

Your

Sigmund

79
To Martha Bernays

Paris
November 24, 1885

My precious sweetheart

. . . Both Mama's and Minna's letters are very nice and require an answer. I am not at all averse to writing and the Republic is pleased that I am in Paris because I spend so much money on stamps. Quite agree about the Christmas present for Frau Gehrke. It is to come from Paris, isn't it?

I am really very comfortably installed now and I think I am changing a great deal. I will tell you in detail what is affecting me. Charcot, who is one of the greatest of physicians and a man whose common sense borders on genius, is simply wrecking all my aims and opinions. I sometimes come out of his lectures as from out of Notre Dame, with an entirely new idea about perfection. But he exhausts me; when I come away from him I no longer have any desire to work at my own silly things; it is three whole days since I have done any work, and I have no feelings of guilt. My brain is sated as after an evening in the theater. Whether the seed will ever bear any fruit, I don't know; but what I do know is that no other human being has ever affected me in the same way. Even old Ricchetti, who has known all the important men of his time, is absolutely bowled over by him. When I get home I feel completely resigned and say to myself: the great problems are for men between fifty and seventy; for young people like us there is Life itself. My ambition would be satisfied by a long life spent learning to understand something of the world, and my plans for the future are that we get married, love each other and work with the object of enjoying life together instead of exerting every ounce of my energy trying to pass the post first, like a race horse—in other words, trying to build myself a home that would involve such effort and privation that I couldn't expect to be granted more than two or three years of mental health. Or am I under the influence of this magically attractive and repulsive city? If so, it would be quite an indirect one. Have you anything to say to this, my darling?

Yesterday I committed a great psychologically interesting blunder. I wanted to buy a *Memoire* by Charcot, which cost 5 francs. But it was out of print, and to own it I would have had to take a volume costing 12 francs from Charcot's Archive. The extra 7 francs struck me as too much. Then the man told me that if I subscribed to Charcot's Archive, I could have all the published works for 60 francs instead of 140. The annual subscription itself is 20 francs. This I did and thus spent 80 francs, ostensibly to save 80 francs. For me the Archive is of the greatest value, but I shall feel the loss of 80 francs. So if you find it so touching that I put away every day a little something for Christmas, just remember this wild extravagance of mine.

Thursday, November 26

My sweet darling

As a result of my monumental laziness and in spite of my persistent desire to write you a long letter, this page has been lying around for two days and you will now receive two letters by one mail, but this is something I don't intend to repeat.

As long as you are well, my darling, I am only too glad not to be the King of Spain. He is the first sovereign of my own generation whom I have outlived, and his death has made a great impression on me. The utter absurdity of the hereditary system will once again be proven when, under the rule of a five-year-old queen following the death of one man, the whole country will rise up in arms.—I prefer to rejoice at hearing that Dr. Cohn has done you so much good, for which achievement I consider no price too high. But I feel sure he won't overcharge you. It is about time Minna went to him, too; please insist on it—

Now I must tell you about a second visit I paid yesterday. They wrote me from home that the wife of our family physician, Dr. Kreisler, is in Paris; I should have called on her long ago. I have just been there, Rue Bleue in the Faubourg Poissoniere, next to the Conservatoire. The unfortunate woman has a ten-year-old son who, after two years in the Vienna Conservatorium, won the great prize there and is said to be highly gifted. Now instead of secretly throttling the prodigy, the wretched father, who is overworked and has a house full of children, has sent the boy with his mother to Paris to study at the Conservatoire and try for another prize. Just imagine the expense, the separation, the dispersal of the household! Needless to say the poor woman, who is giving up everything for the boy, is bored to tears. Little wonder that parents grow vain about their children, and even less that such children grow vain themselves. I will have to go and see them at least once a week, first because I feel under an obligation to him, secondly because she is rather in need of my medical attention, and then it seems good diplomacy to remain on pleasant terms with a Viennese colleague. The prodigy is pale, plain, but looks pretty intelligent.

Meanwhile the Archive has arrived and contains highly valuable material, so I don't regret the expense.—Today Charcot announced he was not going to appear, and so instead of the Salpetriere we went to the Louvre, or rather we drove there, for it was raining cats and dogs.

Yesterday evening John came to see me; he sends you his kind regards. He is quite a decent boy. What amused me was that he was evidently trying to sound me out about whether I keep a mistress here. I trust not on your instructions, my little woman? Perhaps it was Mary's curiosity. Or I misinterpreted his rather
naive talk.

Now don't go and pay me back, my darling, and write to me soon again. But you are so good, I needn't have mentioned it. I couldn't possibly regret leaving Paris, for after all I am coming to Hamburg.

With fondest greetings and many kisses, which will be cashed in their own time.

Your
Sigmund

80
To Martha Bernays

Paris, Saturday
December 12, 1885

Dearest highly esteemed little Princess

Does your Highness really believe it is so easy to tear oneself away from Paris? Don't be alarmed, I am arriving in Hamburg on the morning of the twenty-first; this is certain; but I shall hardly see Berlin; I shall return to Paris instead, "What on earth has happened, you crazy man?" Nothing, my little woman, except that Charcot took me aside today and said: *"J'ai* un mot a vous dire." And then he told me he would gladly consent to my translating his Volume III into German—what's more, not only the first section, which has already appeared in French, but also the second, which hasn't yet been published. Are you pleased? I am. This **is** again something very gratifying. It is bound to make me known to doctors and patients in Germany and is well worth the expense of a few weeks and several hundred gulden, not to mention the few hundred gulden it will bring in. It will be of great advantage to my practice and moreover will pave the way for my own book when that is ready for publication.

Ricchetti thinks that this would not be the moment to leave Charcot, when one has just begun to establish a contact with him, and I really do think he is right But this has nothing to do with my being away from here for ten days, except that when I kiss you I will be richer by one prospect. And you really do deserve, my sweet treasure, to be a little pleased with me, considering the times you have had reason to be sad on my account. Well, this was a good day, similar to that which brought me the traveling grant, and I trust you will not advise me against coming to see you before I plunge into my new work in Paris.

Today so far has been like a scene from a comedy in which everything happens at once. Charcot's permission, a good letter from home; Rosa writes that she is terribly busy—my winter coat, my shirts and shoes! What the afternoon has in store I don't know-but I would like to know what happened in your life today.

I shall probably give up my apartment, but I can surely get it back again; my books I will pack away in a box and store it at Ricchetti's. . . .

I feel like shouting and jumping for joy and what I would like best is to be with you already today, my dear, good darling. I hope you agree with my return under these circumstances.

I kiss you many thousand times.

Your

Sigmund

81
To Martha Bernays

Paris
December 18, 1885

My precious darling

Just one more short letter which may perhaps arrive at the same time as myself. I am glad you have abandoned your resistance to my coming. Do you still remember the first compliment I paid to you, the unsuspecting girl, more than *3½* years ago? I said that roses and pearls fall from your lips as with the princess in the fairy tale and that one is left wondering only whether it is goodness or intelligence that has the upper hand with you. This is how you acquired the name of Little Princess. And now that I know you so well I can but uphold the compliment, the aptness of which I could at the time only divine. May things always remain like this between us.

I leave here on Sunday morning at 7:30, and arrive in Hamburg at 6:18. Nothing has happened to change the original arrangements. I am taking with me a traveling bag belonging to the Ricchettis, probably a rug of theirs as well, the small English handbag, nothing else. Box and trunk are packed and will be stored with them.

I am bringing nothing but some candy for the children and some tiny trifles for the rest of you. In Cologne I will also buy a bottle of eau de cologne for Mama. . . .

Yesterday I had one more interview with Charcot, during which he very obligingly yielded to all the demands of the publisher. The whole thing is now safe and settled. I have written to the publisher and expect to receive his offer of a fee in Wandsbek.

Tell Minna from me that whenever we entertain friends, there will always be a place laid for her.

I must stop, darling, it is midnight. The Russian has been here and I have read my opus to him. May love and science never desert?

Your
Sigmund

82
To Martha Bernays

Paris, Wednesday
January 20, 1886

My beloved little woman

I acknowledge with pleasure the open admission of the cardinal baseness of your actions, for tradition has always interpreted a semi confession on the part of a "lady" in this way, and even a beloved fiancée retains enough of the unassailable and unchangeable character of a "lady" for the man who loves her. You will allow me quietly to observe that you have been wrong on almost every point and without good reason, and have paid less attention to the whole business than you usually do to things concerning us both. Furthermore., you must allow me to point out that you could easily have changed everything according to your desire if only you had informed me about it. It is already quite some time now since I have been unyielding toward you, especially in small matters; a man will always get annoyed if his little woman appears to be trying to get her own way by any other than straight means. If she is frank with him he will usually give in. But all this probably concerns only the future, for this time I am willing to believe you didn't do it on purpose. Thus renouncing any further explanations on your part about this matter, unless you feel the need for it, I herewith close this diplomatic incident and return to the familiar *du* of more intimate relations and to the carrying out of my duties as a reporter.

I had meant to write to you at midnight, but couldn't find the matches, and so had to take off my elegant clothes and go to bed by the light of the moon. So let us begin at the beginning. On Saturday Charcot came up to Ricchetti and invited him to dine at his house on Tuesday before leaving. Startled, R. declined, and finally accepted to go after dinner. Then Charcot turned to me and repeated the latter form of invitation, which I accepted with a bow, feeling delighted, What's more, he decided on Sunday at 1:30 as the time to discuss the translation. (I have already told you that I have been to see him and was given ten sheets to start with.) I just want to add what his study looks like. It is as big as the whole of our future apartment, a room worthy of the magic castle in which he lives. It is divided in two, of which the bigger section is dedicated to science, the other to comfort. Two projections from the wall separate the two sections. As one enters one looks through a triple window to the garden; the ordinary panes are separated by pieces of stained glass. Along the side walls of the larger section stands his enormous library on two levels, each with steps to reach the one above. On the left of the door is an immensely long table covered with periodicals and odd books; in front of the window are smaller tables with portfolios on them. On the right of the door is a smaller stained-glass window, and in front of it stand Charcot's writing table, quite flat and covered with manuscripts and books; his armchair and several other chairs. The other section has a fireplace, a table, and cases containing Indian and Chinese antiques. The walls are covered with Gobelins and pictures; the walls themselves are painted terra cotta. The little I saw of the other rooms on Sunday contained the same wealth of pictures, Gobelins, carpets and curios—in short, a museum.

After Charcot had reminded us once more of our appointment on Tuesday morning, we spent all the afternoon preparing for the evening. Ricchetti, who hitherto had been going about in the most incredibly shabby clothes, had been persuaded by his wife to buy a new pair of trousers and a hat; his tailor is said to have told him that for a party it is quite unnecessary to wear a tail coat and that he could go in a redingote, with the result that he was the only guest not in full evening dress. My appearance was immaculate except that I had replaced the unfortunate ready-made white tie with, one of the beautiful black ones from Hamburg. This was my tail coat's first appearance; I had bought myself a new shirt and white gloves, as the washable pair are no longer very nice; I had my hair set and my rather wild beard trimmed in the French style; altogether I spent fourteen francs on the evening. As a result I looked very fine and made a favorable impression on myself. We drove there in a carriage the expenses of which we shared. R. was terribly nervous, I quite calm with the help of a small dose of cocaine, although his success was assured and I had reasons to fear making a blunder. We were the first after-dinner guests and as we had to wait for the others to come from the dining room, we spent the time admiring the wonderful salons. But then they came and we were under fire: M. and Madame Charcot; Mile Charcot; M. Leon Charcot; a young M. Daudet, an unattractive youth, son of Alphonse Daudet; Prof. Brouardel, doctor of forensic medicine, a manly, intelligent head; M. Strauss, an assistant of Pasteur and well known for his work on cholera; Prof. Lepine of Lyons, one of France's most distinguished clinicians, a small sickly man; M. Giles de la Tourette, former assistant to Charcot, now to Brouardel, a true Provencal; a Prof. Brock, *membre de Tlnstitut,* mathematician and astronomer who at once started talking German and turned out to be a Norwegian; then came Charcot's brother, a gentleman who looked like Prof. Vulpian but wasn't, and several others whose names I never learned; also an Italian painter, Toffano. And now you will be anxious to know how I fared in this distinguished company. Very well I approached Lepine, whose work I knew, and had a long conversation with him; then I talked to Strauss and Giles de la Tourette, and accepted a cup of coffee from Mme Charcot; later on I drank beer, smoked like a chimney, and felt very much at ease without the slightest mishap occurring. Indeed, one couldn't help feeling at ease, for the whole atmosphere was so informal and a great deal of attention was paid to us foreigners. Lepine suggested I should join him in Lyons, which I wouldn't mind doing; he asked me a great many questions about the Vienna hospital staff and at one moment I became the center of attention. R. had been paying court to Mademoiselle and Madame and the latter suddenly became full of enthusiasm and announced: "qu'il parle toutes les langues. Et vous, Monsieur?" asked Madame Charcot, turning to me. "German, English, a little Spanish," I replied. "And French only very badly." She found this sufficient, and Charcot added: "Il est trop modeste, il ne lui manque que d'habituer ToreiHe." I then admitted that I often don't understand what has been said until half a minute later, and compared this failing to the symptoms of tabes, which went very well.

These were my achievements (or rather the achievements of cocaine), which left me very satisfied. I also received permission to attend Prof. Brouardel's course in the Morgue, where I have been today. The lecture was fascinating, the subject matter not very suitable for delicate nerves. It is described as the latest murder in every Paris newspaper.

You will probably be as interested in the personalities of Madame and Mile Charcot as in my achievements. The former is small, rotund, vivacious, hair powdered white, amiable, in appearance not very distinguished. The wealth comes from her; Charcot started out quite poor; her father is rumored to be worth countless millions. Mile Charcot is something else: also small, rather buxom, and of an almost ridiculous resemblance to her great father, as a result so interesting that one doesn't ask oneself whether she is pretty or not. She is about twenty, very natural and amiable. I hardly talked to her as I kept to the old gentlemen, but R. spoke to her a lot. She is said to understand English and German. Now just suppose I were not in love already and were something of an adventurer; it would be a strong temptation to court her, for nothing is more dangerous than a young girl bearing the features of a man whom one admires. Then I would become a laughingstock, be thrown out, and would be the richer from the experience of a beautiful adventure. It is better as it is, after all.

I very much wonder, by the way, whether this invitation will be the last. I believe it may, for in fact I owe it to Ricchetti. And now something else. Do you know the old song which goes: "And a little bit of falseness is always involved"?

Do you think I don't know that the parcel is being sent now because it was to include something for Eli, and that you did not tell me about it because you were afraid I would object? And am I to be pleased that you allow me to grow increasingly suspicious and that you won't tell me this simple story? Is that nice of you, my child? Not at all. And now as a punishment, don't leave that little jersey jacket till I return, but buy it at once as I always intended you to. You are not very lucky with subterfuges. One of these subterfuges kept annoying me for almost two years, and I would rather think of you with false teeth in your mouth than one dishonest word.

And now enough, you know I am always inclined to think longer and more intensely about such things than they deserve.

With a fond kiss
Your
Sigmund

83
To Martha Bernays

Paris, Wednesday
February 10, 1886

My lovable darling

What a magic city this Paris is! Shall I start by talking about yesterday or shall I answer your many, many questions? Let me start with yesterday. It was the pleasantest evening I have spent here so far. I arrived very early and at the same time as Charcot himself, but he put me at my ease at once by saying that I had been invited not by him but by Madame. My early arrival gave me the advantage of having Mile and then Madame to myself, Mile was very friendly but, as you will be glad to hear, rather inaccessible. More details later. Madame was soon called away by sounds in the background and said by way of explanation: "C'est lui, il ne sait pas se mettre la cravate lui-meme"! I was delighted to share this failing with the great man. He soon appeared and I had him to myself for a quarter of an hour during which I had the chance of mentioning a number of things: first, the news about the child outpatients, to which he said: "Mais c'est quelque chose"; then about my departure, then about a little theory I have evolved around the case he put at my disposal, which he liked very much; then about the translation, and so on. He remarked that Paris was doing me good and that I had "engraisse." Gradually the guests arrived and we sat down to dinner. Apart from the Charcot family (four in number), there was the sculptor of the recently unveiled statue of Claude Bernard, then Charcot's chief assistant Richet and his wife—the latter in a somewhat denuded state for which, considering her beauty, one could hardly blame her and who, as a matter of fact, sat as silent as a statue—then a M. Mendelssohn, a Jew from Warsaw, who had been Charcot's assistant as well as a pupil of the Berlin physiologists and is now working under enviable conditions with patients at the Salpetriere; a M. Arene, journalist and art historian whose articles I read every day in the papers; M. Toffano, an Italian painter whom I was meeting there for the third time, and myself. I sat next to Mile Charcot; I enclose my place card for our archive. We were not given very much to eat, but each dish was exquisite and accompanied by different wines. The conversation was carried on mostly by Madame; Charcot himself was in a gay mood and the family remarked that he was "aimable." Well, now for Mile. She is twenty years old and, despite her small-ness, very pretty, moves with great ease of course, and her interests seem to be divided between her father and brother. "Si fefcais garson," she said. She obviously takes a serious interest in medicine. I tried my best to be attentive and suggested we carry on our conversation in English, but when she told me that English had been her first language I soon stopped. She has a much older sister but not from the same father; the rest of the meal was taken up by a lively dispute between her and the young Charcot which the old man brought to an end with a good-natured "Assez, Mademoiselle!" When the meal was over I had the honor of leading Mlle back to the drawing room, as M. Richet was too far away. Since the dinner had made me feel at ease, I enjoyed myself very much and talked a lot more with Charcot himself, from whom I also borrowed a book and a magazine. A particularly pleasant event for me was the arrival during the evening of M. Ranvier, the famous histologist, who had given me such a friendly reception in the College de France. I think he spoke to Charcot about me, and I myself had a pleasant talk with him later. My confidence as a judge of human nature received a considerable boost when he confided in me that he would have liked best to be a professor in a small German university—for instance, Bonn—for in a letter to Paneth I had described him as a "German university professor badly translated into French." The party grew larger and larger; the later guests included Cornu, the famous optician, with a truly inspired expression; M. Peyron, director of the Assistance Publique, against whom the students recently instigated a huge scandal, no one knows why; and (prepare for a surprise) Daudet himself. A magnificent face! Small figure, narrow head with a mass of black curly hair, a longish but not typically French beard, fine features, a resonant voice, and very lively in his movements. Mme D. was also there, and never left her husband's side; she is so unbeautiful that one cannot imagine she has ever been any better-looking; a worn face, prominent cheek bones. She was dressed like a very young woman, although her eighteen-year-old son, friend of Charcot's son, was present, Daudet doesn't look a day over forty; he must have married very young.

In short, the evening was very amusing. I left with M. de la Tourette and as late as 12:30 went up to his apartment to fetch a paper he had promised me.

The following day I couldn't help thinking what an ass I am to be leaving Paris now that spring is coming, Notre Dame looking so beautiful in the sunlight, and I have only to say one word to Char-cot and I can do whatever I like with the patients. But I feel neither courageous nor reckless enough to stay any longer.

Next day—yesterday, Wednesday—I had another adventure. The Viennese, a truly dreadful fellow, called for me and we went together to the Salpetriere. The man is a hydrotherapist at Winter-nitz's, and as a result considers himself a great neuropathologist and made all kinds of condescending remarks which I took in my stride, confident of an imminent revenge. He had a letter of introduction to Charcot containing some outrageous flattery: that he had arrived to meet the greatest living physician. From this he had evidently expected I don't know what kind of reception, but I knew it would be rather cool. And indeed, after having received the letter, all Charcot said was "A votre service, Monsieur!" and added: "Vous connaissez M. Freud?" to which we both lowered our heads, he rather taken aback, I silently pleased. Then something else happened.

For a week now there has been a foreigner in the Salpetriere, a definitely Germanic type and yet somehow different; I can't quite make him out. Wednesday is the day we go to the ophthalmological room, and there this foreigner suddenly began behaving with some authority; when he exchanged cards with Charcot's ophthalmologist, the latter became very polite and expressed the hope that Monsieur would often return so that he could learn something from Kim. Whereupon we all began wondering who he might be. Before leaving he came over to us Viennese and said: "I heard you speaking German. I'd like to introduce myself." My *bete noire* exchanged cards with him first and I was .still trying to find mine when the foreigner said: "I am a German, but I emigrated to America long ago." At last I gave him my card, but it happened to be one without an address. He glanced at it and said: "Could you be Dr. F. from Vienna? I've known your name for a long time, from your publications, especially the one on cocaine." I was a little surprised and inquired after his name, which turned out to be Knapp. Now, Knapp is the foremost ophthalmologist in New York, who has also written a lot about cocaine and to whom I once wrote a letter in Keller's name. I greeted him accordingly and my *bete noire* stood there looking rather sheepish, first of all because he had failed to recognize the man, and second because he had again managed to make a fool of himself. When he heard the word *cocaine* mentioned he asked: "Have you also written about cocaine?" Whereupon Knapp replied: "Of course he has, it was he who started it all." This morning my Viennese was much more malleable and talked exclusively of the great practice that awaited me in Vienna.

I have had letters again from both the bookseller and Kassowitz. The former much more affable. K. writes only to say that he doesn't want to influence my choice between Breslau and Berlin, but asks me if it is to be the latter not to mention his name because he is on bad terms with the Berlin pediatricians. I am kept very busy with the case Charcot passed on to me; our association continues to be very satisfactory.

But now it is time to answer your questions, my darling. I don't know anything about the funds of the enterprise; I think it is run privately like the other polyclinic and very likely exists on voluntary contributions. There is no question of remuneration for a director of the department, which doesn't make the position less valuable. The consultations take place in a special room containing among other things electrical equipment; there will be one or two students to keep the records; the consultations are held two or three times a week, unpaid, but in return one has material and if one is a *Dozent* one can lecture on this material, if not at once, then in the winter. Do you understand it now? The chief advantages lie in having access to the material and in the reputation one can acquire in this way as a specialist.

I have never told you about my uncle in Breslau because I never think of him. I have seen him three times in my life, on each occasion for a quarter of an hour. He is a younger brother of my father, a rather ordinary man, a merchant, and the story of his family is very sad. Of the four children only one daughter is normal, and married in Poland- One son is a hydrocephalic and feebleminded; another, who as a young man showed some promise, went insane at the age of nineteen, and a daughter went the same way when she was twenty-odd. I had so completely forgotten this uncle that I have always thought of my own family as free of any hereditary taint. But since 1 have been thinking about Breslau it all came back to me, and I am afraid the fact that one of the sons of the other (very unhappy) uncle in Vienna died an epileptic is something I cannot shift to the mother's side, with the result that I have to acknowledge to a considerable "neuropathological taint/* as it is called. Fortunately, of us seven brothers and sisters there are very few symptoms of this kind to report except that we, Rosa and I (I don't count Emanuel), have a nicely developed tendency toward neurasthenia. As a neurologist I am about as worried by such things as a sailor is by the sea. But you, my darling, must realize that it is your duty to keep your nerves in good condition if the three children, of whom you have been prematurely dreaming, are to be healthy. And if the thought of medicine makes you shudder, darling, I can't blame you, but love me you must nevertheless, and if we get married soon we will be very happy, won't we? These stories are very common in Jewish families. But now that's enough about medicine.

The money situation is easily explained. The three hundred florins which are still outstanding for the translation and which I have meanwhile accepted from Paneth as an advance, were for January and February. So you see that money for traveling and for the month of March will have to come from elsewhere. What you say about the detour round Hamburg is quite right; but are you suggesting that I don't want to see you? I will stay only one day, and Vienna and Hamburg I have traveled through direct. Has your Highness taken that in? Assian, the only one likely to notice my presence, probably won't betray me. The ready money is a very unpleasant chapter, little Princess, but the prospect of having you sit beside me for the whole of one day is a very pleasant one, and on that day I refuse to pay any calls, nor will I allow you to do anything but chatter with me.

Fondest greetings and kisses, my little woman; I am ending on a different day from that on which I began, and tomorrow I expect another letter from you.

Your
Sigmund

84
To Martha Bernays

Berlin, Wednesday
March 10, 1886

My sweet darling

What strange things you have been experiencing and what fascinating letters you are able to write! I take a very warm interest in the fate of the silver snake, and your comment on the sensation of receiving telegrams is really excellent. Fortunately nothing like that is happening here. I am going to take the liberty of being as boring today as I was yesterday; so far no adventure, no thrill, no eclat, as we used to have in Paris. Just quiet work. I have plunged into the translation with something akin to passion because I am afraid of not finishing it, no doubt a quite unreasonable fear. This morning I roused myself to the point of going to the Royal Museum, where I had a brief look at the antique fragments, with deep regret at not being able to understand more about them and with nostalgic memories of the Louvre, which is so much more magnificent and substantial. The most interesting things are of course the Pergamene sculptures, all of them fragments representing the battle between the gods and the giants—tense, dramatic scenes. As my colleague Dr. Türkheim used to say, one can't always be a doctor.

What appeals to me more than the stones, however, are the children in the clinic, who on account of their small format and because they are usually well washed I find more attractive material than the large editions of patients. As long as their brains are free of disease, these little creatures are really charming and so touching when they suffer. I think I would find my way about in a children's practice in no time. A few more months' preparation wouldn't do any harm, but I am afraid this is out of the question; the days of my reckless daring have evaporated. Vienna weighs upon me and perhaps more than is right. I am afraid I am ginning nowadays against my otherwise loyally adhered to principle of not tormenting myself with new situations until I am in the midst of them. But I will conquer my present mood, and then I won't worry about anything till I see with my own eyes the detestable tower of St. Stephen's.

And now once more I have come to the end of my material and I ask you to be very patient with me; I cannot after all initiate you into the secrets of children's diseases, and even Baginsky doesn't seem to me a sufficiently important figure to warrant a detailed description. I am secretly counting the days, but you don't have to know the number I have got to.

With fondest greetings and kisses

Your
Sigmund

85
To Martha Bernays

Berlin, Friday
March 19, 1886

My sweet darling

Nothing new has happened; I am annoyed that I am not on my way to you. They have left me in peace so far, and it may turn out that I was afraid of an unloaded gun. Now I shall have to endure it for another week, but then there will be a few lovely days; perhaps by that time it will be possible to travel without the danger of snowdrifts.

I am so industrious, organized, brave, and sober that I am almost worried; no adventure of any kind comes my way. What else have I to tell you except that I had a letter from L. in Breslau asking me to look up his sister-in-law and a *Sanitatsrat* who is also related to him. Well, I suppose I must. But I am rather stingy with my time; I Have never enjoyed work so much. I have been left with such a friendly, edifying memory of Charcot, in its way not unlike the one I had after the ten days with you. I feel I have experienced something precious that cannot be taken away from me. I feel increasingly self-confident, more urbane, more adroit in dealing with colleagues. It is a pity I cannot stay here to take part in the so-called holiday course which begins on the twenty-second. Oh, my little darling, you have but one minor fault: you never win the lottery. Just now I feel so ready to be very happy. I would stay here a few more weeks, then I would get an apartment in Vienna, and we could still get married in the spring, and then together we could practice the skill in traveling which I have acquired during the past seven months. What a pity this must remain a dream! And now I am regretting all the kisses I could have had tomorrow and the day after! But just you wait, I won't let you off these two days, and if you are naughty I will stay longer. A return ticket to Hamburg is valid for more than five days.

I hope Assian came to congratulate you on Saturday morning. He was supposed to announce my arrival, but as I couldn't come I didn't want to call everything off. I wonder if you have been racking your brains as to who sent the bouquet. And why? Perhaps you thought it was Hugo Kadisch[3] trying to bring about a pleasant end to an old relationship.

Threatened by the illustrious visitor, I have decided to get my already rather shapeless French beard (which, by the way, is generally envied here) trimmed. Filled with understandable suspicion of the Berlin scissors, I went to the most fashionable barber, the Court Hairdresser in the Unter den Linden, paid one reichs-mark, and the man (who looked like a cabinet minister) did a bad job. I don't think that's nice.

On Saturday or Sunday I am going to the theater out of gray, grim despair. Not even a library is open on Sunday. And although translating is quite a nice way of spending a Sunday, I have grown quite stupid; I no longer know how to spell or how to insert relative clauses; in my ears nothing seems to sound German or French any more.

"How different it was in France!" I sighed like a Maria Stuart among neuropathologists.

A human being can really go a long way in the art of self-persuasion. If I had had to travel from Paris to Vienna, I think I would have died en route. And now I have reached the point of actually looking forward to Vienna, especially to one thing: to the hours I am going to spend finishing my paper in Obersteiner's lovely library in Dobling.

Do you know what I have just come to realize very clearly? That if life in Vienna is to be at ah humanly possible, I must have one or two thousand florins, and that to acquire this sum people to whom one pays interest will have to be found. Not usurers, needless to say. But where can semi-unselfish capitalists be found willing to lend money at a normal rate of interest with no more guarantee than a human head and two hands? This is the great problem that has to be solved, not at once but in two months' time when my present wretched thousand florins have come to an end, I dare say greater revolutions have taken place in the world than that a man who has nothing now, later acquires a few thousand gulden. I have very little fear of the future. In any case, and this comes first among the achievements of this year of travel: I am coming to fetch you like an overdue bill of exchange on June 15, 1887—if this hasn't been possible before. Are you absolutely determined to be ready by then, my little girl?

Answer verbally at the end of the month to

Your

Sigmund

86
To Martha Bernays

Berlin, Tuesday
March 30, 1886

My sweet darling

If I ever have to leave Wandsbek again without you, I will certainly let you see me off at the station. I very nearly turned about at Schadendorf and came back to spend another night, but I felt a little ashamed, for up to now we really have managed to be pretty sensible at our partings. But this was a very difficult one for me, my darling; and you too, my treasure, shed some tears, and this hurt me to see. But now I really will go ahead, as you suggest, so that you may be spared many more partings and a long period of waiting.

And here I am again in Berlin and we are already as far apart as if I were in Vienna. A new era is beginning, a good one I hope, one that will bring good things. My sweet treasure, I just can't imagine what it will be like when I don't have to leave you any more, and yet I know that I won't be in the least surprised and will feel as if we had always been together.

This time no letter had arrived before me; the journey was very pleasant; I slept nearly the whole night under cover of my knitted rug. I am not in the least tired and am just off to the Cafe Bauer. Don't forget, my little Princess, that you have promised me to keep well and write again soon. 1 too have more time again now that the translation has come to an end.

With lots and lots of kisses, for which a new account begins today.

Your
Sigmund

Fond greetings to Mama and Minna.

87
To Martha Bernays

Vienna, Thursday
May 6, 1886

My sweet girl

Warmest thanks for your dear letter and for the parcel, the contents of which I knew so well I felt I had been present at the purchase. I have always wanted a clytliia and I realize that you knew it. But that you apologize for your gift, dearest, really is unnecessary, and I feel quite ashamed when I think that I am now in your debt instead of competing with you in giving presents. I am now so old, as you know, and yet on the I of the fourth anniversary of our engagement we still don't know when the married state which we have so often visualized will become a reality. But although still as far as ever from the goal, we are less far from the certainty. In a few weeks the money—which I still haven't touched—will have come to an end., and then we shah see whether I can go on living in Vienna. I would like to think that the next birthday will be just as you describe it, that you will be waking me up with a kiss and I won't be waiting for a letter from you. I really no longer care where this will be, whether here or in America., Australia or anywhere else. But I don't want to be much longer without you. I can put up with any amount of worry and hard work, but no longer alone. And between ourselves, I have very little hope of being able to make my way in Vienna.

I am continuing this in the evening, darling. There were two old patients of Breuer's at my consultation today, no one else. I usually have five: two for electric treatment, one for nothing, one *schnorrer* and *one—schadchen.*

Then came the congratulations: Pauli and Dolfi brought me a beautiful little brush box, Mitzi a large photograph of herself and two Makart bouquets, Mother a cake and Rosa a lovely framed blotter for my writing table. There were written congratulations from Willenz, Schani, Kleinenberger and Uncle Elias, whom I want you to thank very much for me. So they celebrated me like a prince; I have every reason to be tired and am going to bed early.

Work in the laboratory is giving me great pleasure. I certainly have time enough. I also have another therapeutic idea, which I shall try out very soon. But it is rather doubtful that it will prove as valuable as the coca one.

Goodnight, my little woman. Here's to next year!

Your
Sigmund

I'll write to Mama and Minna separately tomorrow.

88
To Martha Bernays

Vienna, Thursday
May 13, 1886

My beloved darling

I won't be able to write to you any more during my consulting hours because there is too much going on. The waiting room is full of people and I shall hardly be finished by three o'clock. The takings are not yet very brilliant, but the patients who avail themselves of my services are quite numerous, though there aren't many paying ones among them: Frau Prof. M, who gives me a lot of trouble, the sciatica is which is almost cured, and the two police officials who come once a week. Tomorrow T. is coming. Today my earnings amounted to eight florins: three from a police official and live again through Breuer, who sent Frau Dr. K. She came to ask for some advice to relieve her husband.

I realize that for a doctor work and income are two very different things. Sometimes one makes money without lifting a finger, at other times one slaves away without reward. The day before yesterday, for instance, an American physician came to see me with a nervous complaint—a complicated case which interests me so much that I took it on without getting anything out of it. His case is complicated by his relationship with his beautiful and interesting wife with whom I also have to deal and on whose account I am going to see Prof. Ghrobak tomorrow. I am too tired to describe to you in detail ah[1] the delicate aspects. It seemed weird to me that on both the occasions she was here your photograph, which has otherwise never budged, fell off the writing table. I don't like such hints, and if a warning were needed—but none is needed.

And a doctor is supposed to economize! Here I am counting every gulden and I am called to go and see a distant acquaintance in the Stadtgutgasse, no remuneration of course, and two hours out of the day gone, for I cannot afford a cab. Today the same. When I get home I find an urgent message to go and see the man again. This time of course I am obliged to take a cab, and what I have saved in suppers during the past three days has to be spent on it.

On Tuesday I gave a lecture in the Physiological Club on hypnotism; it went off very well and received general applause. I have announced the same lecture for two weeks from today in the Psychiatric Club, and during the next three weeks I will give another lecture on my Paris experiences before the Medical Association. So the battle of Vienna is in full swing, and if you were here I would tell you with a kiss that I haven't abandoned the hope of calling you my wife in six months.

I think I will have to arrange for a second consulting hour three times a week from three to four for nonpaying patients and those in need of slight electrical treatment. In spite of everything my position here is a strong one, as I can see from several indications.

Goodnight, my sweet darling.

Your
Sigmund

What do you think of a collective present for Mama again this year?

89
To Martha Freud

Vienna IX, Berggasse 19
Thursday, June 7, 1894

My beloved darling

Yesterday evening was almost unbearably sultry. In the morning I wake at six, find the room light, think to myself that this rare event of waking up so early should be put to some use, knock at Marie's door and order a bath, then lie down again. Half an hour later I wake up again, find the room so dark that I can't see the clock quickly dismisses the notion that I could have gone blind, dash to the window and see a strip of black sky. A few minutes later comes, a roar of thunder, in no time the street is completely white, horses break loose, hailstones of a fantastic size beat against the windows. I rush to the back, there I find the study window already smashed in three places, the writing table flooded, the wings of the window wide open, of course. The terrace looked almost grandiose, the doors had been blown open and the hailstones covered the floor as far as the sideboard. The storm lasted for half an hour. The devastation in the city is terrific. On one side of almost every street (in the Berggasse it's opposite) nearly all the windowpanes are smashed, especially in the upper stories; for long stretches not one pane is intact, as though boys had bombarded them with stones; at street corners and where windows have not been protected by moldings it looks simply ludicrous. A woman who came to see me this morning was quite right when she said that the windows looked like circus hoops after dogs had jumped through them. Other streets have been spared. The trees have suffered most; in our garden there are more leaves on the ground than on the branches, and the poor tree itself is torn and battered; it looks as though it had been thrashed with whips and then chewed by caterpillars. Anything that was a garden must be in an awful state. I am told that the windows—in our case only one—are to be repaired by the landlord. I am anxious to know if you had anything like this in your part of the world; it could have been quite a mess. I hope not, and that it was only local.

No news otherwise. Yesterday I did my writing in the evening and hope to do the same today. Business middling; today it would be more profitable to be a glazier than a doctor.

Fond greetings
Your
Sigmund

90
To Martha Freud

Venice, on board, en route to the Lido
Tuesday morning
August 27. 1895

My precious darling

We agreed that you won't get many detailed descriptions. The trance which Venice puts everyone into makes it impossible. We are enormously well and spend all day walking, cruising, gazing, eating, and drinking. Every morning to the Lido, twenty minutes, to bathe in the sea, the most delicious sand underfoot Yesterday was cool and the sea rather rough; today has started hot. Yesterday we also went up the tower of St. Mark's, strolled from the Rialto through the town, which allows one to see the strangest things, visited a church, Frari, and the Scuola S. Rocco, enjoyed a surfeit of Tintorettos, Titians, and Canovas, went four times to the Cafe Quadri on the piazza, wrote letters, entered into negotiations about some purchases, and the two days seem like six months. *Zanzare* definitely exist. Needless to say, I am already very anxious to hear your news. The only letter so far is from Minna, *paste restante. I* hope you and ah[1] the brats are very well.

Fond greetings
Your
Sigmund

91
To Martha Freud

Rome,
September 21, 1907

E quindi uscimmo a riveder le stele.

Who know this? Until nightfall I was with the dead in a Roman columbarium, in Christian and Jewish catacombs. It is cold, dark and not very pleasant down there. In the Jewish ones the inscriptions are Greek, the candelabrum-I think it's called Menorah-can be seen on many tablets. The (female) guide-I was the only visitor-forgot to bring the key of the exit, so we had either to go all the way back or stay down below. I chose the former.

Affectionately

Papa

92
To Martha Freud

Vienna IX, Berggasse 19
April 29, 1908

My beloved Old Dear,

I am very pleased that you found Mama so much better than you expected; this gives your journey quite a different character.

The congress was a great success and I think it has left a good impression on all those who took part in it. For me it has meant a great deal of work, but without result. While we were having dinner on Monday I happened to glance behind me into the hall and saw a back that struck me as familiar, unlikely though the meeting seemed. I rushed to inspect the back from the front and sure enough it was Emanuel, who was revenging himself in this way for the surprise in Wiesbaden. We met again, the following morning when everyone had left, and in the evening he took me to the station. The hours between we spent talking and drinking beer-mostly he-went up to the Fortress, to Hellbrunn, and so on. For serventy-five he is amazingly vigorous, but for the first time he showed definite signs of having aged; the last bout of influenza has taken it out of him. He was on his way to Berlin, was very interested to hear about Mama, and was as aghast about Rosa as we all are.

There were more patients today at consultation than I could deal with. Tomorrow an Englishman and an American are coming to dinner.

Ford greetings

Yours
Sigmund

Sweet Memories of
Freud

Martha Bernays (1861-1951), in 1882 four years
prior to her 1886 marriage to Sigmund Freud.

Sigmund Freud (1856-1939), and his fiancee Martha Bernays in June 1885, a year before their marriage.

Sigmund Freud and Martha
after Wedding-1886

Sigmund Freud (1856-1939), at age 45 in 1909, the year
he traveled to the United States to lecture. The following
year he published THE ORIGIN AND DEVELOPMENT OF
PHYCHOANALYSIS, a popular book that explained his
theories to a board audience.

Sigmund Freud (1856-1939), standing on sidewalk outside The Hague, Netherlands, 1920.

Sigmund Freud (1856-1939) smoking cigar in a classic
early 1920s portrait.

Sigmund Freud | Oct. 27, 1924 on TIME Cover

Sigmund Freud (1856-1939), and his mother, Amalia
Freud (1835-1929), in 1925.

Sigmund Freud, with his sons, Ernst and Martin who were serving in the Austrian Army during World War I. The violence of the war affected Freud's ideas, later to be expressed in CIVILIZATION AND ITS DISCONTENTS published in 1930.

Vienna, Austria 1936Professor Sigmund Freud at his home with his dogs in Vienna on his 80th birthday.

Sigmund Freud seated in his study contemplating a carved
figurine (possibly Javanese) on his desk in 1937
photography by Princess Marie Bonaparte.

Sigmund Freud, seated in his study with his dog in 1937
photography by Princess Marie Bonaparte who founded
the French Institute of Psychoanalysis in 1926.

The couch in the consulting room of Sigmund Freud's office in Vienna as it looked in 1938, before his emigration to England when Germany annexed Austria.

Sigmund Freud (1856-1939), with his "secret committee" of six
loyal supporters. Seated (left to right) Freud, Sandor Ferenczi,
and Hans Sachs. Standing (left to right) Otto Rank, Karl Abraham, Max Eitingon, and Ernest Jones.

Sigmund Freud (1856-1939), with Marie Bonaparte and
U.S. Ambassador William C. Bullitt, arriving in Paris
enroute to England. Princess Marie Bonaparte paid Freud's
ransom to Nazis, enabling him to leave Austria.

Bibliography

References

- A Patel, (2013) "Person of Issue: Sigmund Freud (1856-1939)", The International Journal of Indian Psychology: Volume: 01, Issue: 01, October-December 2013, Pg 1 to 8
- Ernest Jones, The Life and Work of Sigmund Freud (1964) p. 109. 116-9, and p. 133 Bakan, 57, 196.
- Ernest Jones, The Life and Work of Sigmund Freud (1964) p. 110-1 and p. 165-6
- Ernst L. Freud (1960) "Letters of Sigmund Freud" Basic Books Inc., Publishers, New York,
- Sigmund Freud. (2015). The Biography.com website. Retrieved 12:01, Jul 19, 2015, from http://www.biography.com/people/sigmund-freud-9302400.

Webs

- http://freudfile.org/
- http://pixgood.com/sigmund-freud-drawing.html
- http://ijip.in

A Big Hug to…

- Sigmund Freud Museum, London
- Basic Books Inc, New York
- The International Journal of Indian Psychology, India
- Amazon, India, USA
- RED'SHINE Publication, India
- ASF Computer Un. Ltd, India
- Bhaikaka Library, Sardar Patel University, India
- Department of Psychology, Sardar Patel University, India
- RED'SHINE Studios. Inc, India
- RED'MAGIC Networks. Inc, India
- Dot'Red, Inc, India

www.ingramcontent.com/pod-product-compliance
Lightning Source LLC
Chambersburg PA
CBHW080408290526

45791CB00008BA/2188